Rabaul

C. Lambert

Kokopo

NEW
IRELAND

St. Georges Channel

C. St.
George

Sea

Kimbe Bay

Crater
Pt.

Tolokiwa
Id.

C. Gloucester

Talasea

Pomio

Umbol Id.

Dampier Strait

Sagsag

Atiatu

NEW BRITAIN

Iungpun

Strait

Kumbun

Au

ab

Arawe

Kandrian

Apugi

Gasmata

Finschhafen

C. Cretin

olo

Huon
Gulf

Solomon   Sea

Morobe

Manau

vera

Ambasi

Trobriand
Is.

indewari

Sangara

Agenehambo

Gona

Sasembata

Buna

t.Lamington

Popondetta

Kokoda

Ilegaraja

Oro Bay

Sefoa

Eroro

Tufi

Goodenough
Id.

Sila

Waṅigela

Woodlark Id.

OWEN

Safia

Tarakwaruru

Fergusson
Id.

STANLEY

Uiaku

Menapi

RA.

Abau

Agaun

Boianai

Normanby
Id.

Hood Pt.

Dogura

Taupota

East C.

Samarai

Misima
Id.

South C.

148°   150°   152°

THE ROAD FROM GONA

*Dorothea Tomkins
and Brian Hughes*

THE ROAD
FROM GONA

ANGUS AND ROBERTSON

First published in Great Britain in 1970 by
ANGUS & ROBERTSON LTD
54 Bartholomew Close, London
221 George Street, Sydney
107 Elizabeth Street, Melbourne
65 High Street, Singapore

283·95
T595   180447

ISBN 0 207 95189 6

Registered in Australia for transmission by post as a book
PRINTED IN AUSTRALIA BY HALSTEAD PRESS, SYDNEY

Foreword

DOROTHEA TOMKINS served on the staff of the Diocese of New Guinea from 1937 to 1967. During the war years she was in the area invaded by the Japanese. Eventually, with Mrs R. L. Newman and Mrs Dennis Taylor and children she walked over the Owen Stanley Range to safety in the south. In 1963 she wrote the story of the lives of the New Guinea Martyrs. She had known them personally as fellow workers. Indeed she had been one of those who had stayed on the job as they had. She might well have been caught and executed with them. Her story as written was full of fragrant personal memories and anecdotes retailed by relatives and other friends.

Brian Hughes left the New South Wales Education Department in 1962 to join the staff of the Martyrs Memorial School, Agenehambo. He interested himself in the development of the school and soon realized the need for a written history of the origins and early years. His research led him to the Martyrs themselves. After a considerable effort of searching out the living who could remember the dead, and after comparing notes with Dorothea Tomkins, he wrote an account of the events leading up to the deaths as far as it was possible to reconstruct from disjointed and incomplete sources. His work is incorporated in an academic thesis as yet incomplete.

The manuscripts of Dorothea Tomkins and Brian Hughes were shown to the Australian Board of Missions and aroused immediate interest. There had long been a demand for a full account of the New Guinea martyrdoms. A.B.M. asked L. C. Rodd to compile a single-volume account based on the work of Dorothea Tomkins and Brian Hughes.

This book now published is the compilation written by L. C. Rodd. He has incorporated the text of the other manuscripts in some sections and in other places he has recast their story to fit the over-all perspective which the A.B.M. asked him to adopt.

He has consulted many other sources. He has spread the net of the story back to the beginnings of the mission and forward to 1968. In doing this he has shown for the first time in one story how the missionaries who stayed and died were fulfilling the ministry of all who had served in New Guinea. He has gone on to show how they opened the gate to a future in which Papuans, New Guineans, Melanesians and Europeans working and suffering together are finding together that joy in the Lord which is a secret of the Church.

FRANK W. COALDRAKE

Sydney
February 1969

Chairman,
Australian Board of Missions.

Contents

Illustrations

I

The Pioneers

THE old man pointed to the ring of stones above the beach between Wamira and Kaieta. "The councillors were seated there when they came," he said. "I was a boy, but my father was of the council. The boat came round the point, three white men and a Samoan. The Councillors voted whether they should be killed. My father — he was with those who said No."

Bernard of Wamira, eighty-five years old, is one of three still living who saw the landing of the first Anglican missionaries on Kaieta beach. The Anglican Mission to New Guinea had been given a mandate, a spiritual sphere of influence, from Milne Bay along the north coast to the borders of German New Guinea. From the time of that first landing on 10th August 1891, for the lifetime of the oldest man, it was responsible for the medical, educational and social welfare of the Papuan people north of the Owen Stanley Range. Its stations were reached only by the mission's vessels or by tracks such as the road from Gona built across swamps into the interior.

Cut off from the administrative centre of Port Moresby by the Owen Stanleys, the Anglican Mission area lay to the south-east of Lae and Salamaua by which traders, explorers and anthropologists entered northern New Guinea to follow the trails to the highlands. The history of the Anglican Mission, little known, is a record of courage and hardship in natural disaster and continuing difficulty, of heroism and sacrifice in peace and war.

It was for Albert Maclaren and Copland King the Feast of St

Laurence when they landed at Kaieta. The two missionaries had sailed from Cooktown, Queensland, in the *Grace Lynn*, a small schooner they had chartered for three months or longer. The passage had been a rough one; but, leaving the *Grace Lynn* at Samarai, the two men had pushed on in a whaleboat manned by a white navigator and eight Papuan natives. Rain poured down all night of the night of 8th August, and the party camped uncomfortably on the damp bottom of the boat with the sails spread overhead as an awning. The next day the eight natives left to go to their village and the three white men and a Samoan boy continued on into Bartle Bay past Cape Frere. The surf was too violent for them to land that evening and they spent another uncomfortable night with the boat "rolling terribly" a little way off the beach.

On the morning of 10th August they woke to see a large group of natives lining the beach. After a great deal of chattering, one of these set out to the whaleboat in a catamaran. Maclaren stepped onto the platform, but his weight capsized it and he went under. The native swam back to the shore and Maclaren, who could not swim, was in some danger of drowning for the others in the boat were preparing breakfast under the awning and had not seen the capsize.

A little later the whaleboat was backed onto the beach, and the missionaries were well received by a group of about forty of the leading men. Maclaren made a present of tobacco to a man he thought to be the chief — a handful of sticks for himself and the rest to be shared among the others. With an escort of twenty natives the two missionaries walked through the village of Wedau, and, carried across a stream by the natives, they made their way through long grass to the top of the hill of Dogura, an ancient battleground, which was to be the head-station of the Anglican Mission in New Guinea.

The hill was two hundred and twelve feet high, with steep sloping banks on three sides, and backed by mountains on the fourth. "It is on this plateau that we decided to build our house," wrote Copland King. "There is plenty of room for a plantation around it and on the hillsides, while the view from it embraces Cape Frere and Bartle Bay to the east, the level lowland below, hemmed in by mountains, some of them rising to five and six thousand feet, with watercourses shining on their sides."

In the evening Maclaren and Copland King went down to the village of Wedau, gathered a hundred or so of the Papuans, and tried to explain — without an interpreter — what they wished to do for them. The singing of a native hymn was more successful. Four years before, Dr Chalmers ("Tamate") of the London Missionary Society had explored the coast from the Gulf of Papua to Milne Bay, and melodies of native hymns of the L.M.S were known to natives untouched by the Society's teaching.

The London Missionary Society had been established at Port Moresby since 1874; the Roman Catholic Church had formed a mission settlement on Yule Island, to the west of Port Moresby; and, following the proclamation of Papua as a British protectorate in 1888, the Methodist Church was given, as a missionary sphere, the majority of the outlying islands. When Albert Maclaren made a preliminary visit to New Guinea in 1890 it was decided at a friendly conference that the Church of England should be allowed to operate exclusively on the north-east coast of Papua from Cape Ducie to Mitre Rock.

The landing at Kaieta and the decision to set up a mission station on Dogura Hill were for Albert Maclaren the climax to years of preparation. He had sought to join the Universities Mission to Central Africa but was rejected by the doctors. He came to Australia, received Holy Orders, and served for nine years in Queensland and New South Wales. This experience had been good training for a pioneer missionary. In his first sermon at Mackay he told his congregation, "You starved out one man, you broke another man's heart, and you drove another man away. Now the Roman Catholic priest will always give me an old coat, the Methodist minister will give me a meal, so you can't starve me out, you can't break my heart, and you can't drive me away, for I don't mean to go."

His own property — and that of others — was always at the disposal of the needy. He arrived at a station drenched by rain and the squatter lent him a new suit. He went home in it, put it in a drawer and forgot it until a needy tramp arrived at the rectory door. Going to his wardrobe, he told the tramp, "I quite forgot I had these. They must be clothes I had when I was a layman. Take them." The squatter later asked for the return of his suit and was upset by its loss. Maclaren replied, "I had forgotten they were yours. But really the man was much worse off than you are."

In 1889 he was accepted by Bishop Barry, then Primate of Australia, as the first missionary of the Church of England in New Guinea. In 1890 he was in Papua preparing the way for the establishment of the mission, acting as private secretary to the Governor, travelling about, observing native customs. He was at Thursday Island when the Royal Mail steamer *Quetta* with 291 people aboard struck an uncharted rock on the night of 28th February 1890 and sank within three minutes. Maclaren found a place aboard the rescue ship *Albatross* and, while comforting the mourners and helping the survivors, he visualized the erection of a memorial church on Thursday Island which would become a centre for missionary activity. He wrote to the Queensland newspapers explaining his proposal on 26th April 1890. Within a short time £2,000 was raised and portion of the church consecrated in 1893. Seven years later the Quetta Memorial Church became the cathedral church of the first Bishop of Carpentaria, Gilbert White.

From September 1890 to July 1891 Maclaren was travelling the length of Australia striving to raise the necessary money for the New Guinea Mission. He found it "weary work, waiting about and begging for money". Offered "the surplus offertory" by an archdeacon a hundred miles from Melbourne, he travelled out to find that the incumbent had gone away, leaving him single-handed to cope with the services and miscellaneous duties of the parish. To collect the purchase money for the whaleboat he had to make a special trip to Hobart and Launceston. He was trying to gather together a staff, arrange for building material, charter a hundred-ton collier schooner. It was little wonder he wrote to his mother that he would be "quite glad to get to New Guinea".

It has been asked why it was necessary for Maclaren to exhaust himself in this single-handed drudgery before he began his great adventure. The Bishop of Melbourne had already warned the Australian Church "If you don't send your men and money to New Guinea, other branches of the Church will not, and the work, left for you to do, will be left undone."

Maclaren was a High Church man — "more a Catholic, so they tell me, than I am myself", said Bishop Verjus, the lovable leader of the Sacred Heart Mission on Yule Island. Yet on his visit to Port Moresby, Maclaren formed a warm friendship with Dr Lawes, the veteran missionary of the London Missionary

Society, and with members of the Wesleyan Mission. Long before the days of ecumenism he prayed in the Chapel of the Sacred Heart Mission when he found Bishop Verjus sick in bed with fever. And he warmed the hearts of the Congregationalists of the L.M.S. and the Methodists by joining not only in their family worship but in their communion service. "Am I not right?" he reflected. "Surely in a heathen country we don't want to shock the poor natives by our unhappy divisions. God listens to us all. I trust I am none the less a Catholic in the deepest sense."

Two days after Maclaren and Copland King reached Kaieta, the *Grace Lynn* arrived in Bartle Bay and anchored a quarter of a mile from Wedau beach. "A hundred and twelve pounds of trade tobacco, ten tomahawks, ten large and ten small knives, twenty-four looking-glasses, some red Turkey twill, beads, twenty-five pipes, and a few boxes of matches" were handed over on Dogura Hill to the native owners, the purchase of two hundred and sixty acres being afterwards confirmed by the government.

The next four and a half months saw the establishment of the Anglican Mission at Dogura. A cart-horse — an "enormous pig" to the natives — had been brought on the *Grace Lynn* and helped to some degree in the conveyance of stores. But the entire population of the villages of Wedau and Wamira turned out to help the missionaries. There were sometimes as many as two hundred men working at once. A temporary living-house was built at once of rough tree-trunks and grass, and the material for a large European house was landed from the schooner and taken up the hill. But for weeks the white men were living on the *Grace Lynn*, their blankets drenched every time it rained. "Last night," wrote Maclaren, "we had three inches of rain under our beds, the water having soaked in all round."

Maclaren supervised the building of drains on Dogura Hill, the erection of a chapel. Coconut-trees were planted for the future. Daily visits were paid to the villages and services held on Sundays. Meanwhile he was working hard to acquire a vocabulary of several hundred words of the native language. The villagers of Boianai and Radava, sixteen miles away, sent messages to the people of Wedau that they were coming to attack them and kill the missionaries. Maclaren asked some of the chiefs of Wedau and Wamira to go with him in the whaleboat to Boianai. He landed alone and went straight to the village. Presents were exchanged, and Maclaren made friends with the people. A few days later came news that a chief man at Boianai had been killed by people from Radava. Maclaren again went to Boianai, this time to join with the people in their mourning, to comfort them with presents, and to find the murderer.

He was visiting the villages round Cape Frere when he was struck down by fever. He had had no opportunity to become acclimatized. He was travelling by day under a tropical sun and sleeping at night in the native club houses, where scores of young Papuan men lay thickly pressed round him on the shingle. On 14th December he set out in the whaleboat for Samarai. "I must make a move tonight," he wrote, "calling at Taupota, Awaiama, and other places on the way, as I am anxious to visit all the villages between here and Cape Ducie before Christmas."

The voyage was a hard one and he was often seasick. At Samarai he was carried aboard the *Merrie England* almost delirious. Sir Samuel Griffith, Premier of Queensland, was on the ship and he decided that Maclaren's only chance was to be taken to Cooktown. Maclaren was carried aboard on 26th December and died the following morning. He was thirty-eight years old.

The tomb of Albert Alexander Maclaren was for years in Cooktown cemetery. On it was inscribed: "A Missionary Priest by whose faith and zeal the New Guinea Mission was founded. *Miles Christi.*" The stone collapsed and the grave remained neglected until years later when the remains of Albert Maclaren were reinterred in Dogura Cathedral.

While Maclaren was lecturing through New South Wales in 1890 the train in which he was travelling was shortened at Singleton and he was placed in a carriage with the Reverend Copland King. The two men talked together and King explained that he was interested in the New Guinea Mission; his Sunday school collected for it, and he had heard Maclaren speak at a meeting in Sydney.

At Quirindi they left the train together and walked the streets until Maclaren suggested they call on a bachelor known to him. As his hand was raised to knock on the door a voice inside asked, "What shall it be, nap or euchre?" With a smile Maclaren said, "I don't think we're wanted here", and the two resumed their tramp along the dusty road. It was then that Maclaren asked, "How about you coming to New Guinea?"

*The Reverend Albert Maclaren,
pioneer Anglican missionary
and co-founder of the
New Guinea Mission.*

*The Reverend Copland King,
pioneer Anglican missionary
and co-founder of the
New Guinea Mission.*

Mavis Parkinson, teacher at Gona, martyred August 1942.

Sister Margery Brenchley, nurse at Sangara, martyred August 1942.

Lilla Lashmar, teacher at Sangara, martyred August 1942.

Sister May Hayman, nurse at Gona, martyred August 1942.

The Reverend Vivian Redlich, priest at Sangara, martyred August 1942.

Copland King was an evangelical, the son of an archdeacon, a Master of Arts, and later to receive for his work on Papuan languages the degree of Th.Soc. Maclaren recognized in him the man he needed. "I will do the work," he told King, "But I want a university man to learn the language, compile the grammar and give us the books." (The two men were united in their desire that the mission should be above "party" spirit and should command the sympathy and support of the whole Church.)

They had been together in New Guinea for only a few months when Maclaren recognized that Copland King's chances of recovering from fever were receding and sent him to Sydney ostensibly on mission business, but with a request to the Primate* that King should not be allowed to return until he had regained complete health. After Maclaren's death the Primate, on 16th March 1892, appointed Copland King head of the New Guinea Mission.

Meanwhile at Dogura three lay missionaries, Mr and Mrs Tomlinson and Mr Kennedy, were holding the mission together. A fortnight after Christmas they heard of Maclaren's death. "Now all we can do is await the arrival of the new head, and while waiting work away at the language." To this was added the digging of drains, making of paths, erection of a boathouse, planting of a vegetable garden, and attempts to get the children of the villages to come to school. Their spirit was in contrast to that of the Sydney newspaper which summed up the work of the New Guinea Mission as — *nil*.

On the morning of Low Sunday 1892 Copland King arrived at Dogura with two carpenters he had brought from Brisbane. Within a month he was sailing the coast in the whaleboat seeking a site for a second mission station, exploring the inland, visiting villages where murders had taken place, in efforts to hold back raids of retaliation.

In 1893 he was conferring with the L.M.S. and Wesleyan missionaries at Kwato, westward from Samarai. The conference made recommendations to the government about the laws of marriage, adultery and divorce among natives. It was decided that the Lord's name in all missions should be *Iesu Keriso*.

Classes were started in the villages, but the languages remained

*The Most Reverend William Saumarez Smith, Archbishop of Sydney.

B

the great barrier. On Whitsunday 1896 occurred the first
Baptisms, and one of those baptized was Selwin, a native boy to
whom King had been accustomed to read over the English of the
Gospel, explaining it as far as possible. Selwin would render this
in the Wedauan dialect. The two would discuss the translation
before writing it down. There would be further discussions and
then King would read the translation to another native for
criticism. Finally the whole was written down for the press.

From the start an attempt was made to give regular schooling
to the children at Wedau. Since they could not be persuaded to
come every day to Dogura, Copland King went down the hill each
morning to Wedau, and one of the laymen to Wamira. The
children were gathered under a tree, and school was held. It
seemed a wonderful achievement when they could "just manage
to say the alphabet". School was followed by visiting in the
village and by attention to the sick.

Copland King was to spend twenty-seven years in Papua. In
the last years of the nineteenth century, while he was head of the
New Guinea Mission, he saw the welcome arrival of other missionaries, the extension of mission stations along the coast to
Awaiama, Taupota, Boianai and Menapi. He saw the coming
of the white gold prospectors and faced the consequences of their
encounters with the natives. He saw the foundations of the
Anglican Mission established to the degree that Sir William
MacGregor was writing in his Call to the Church: "Mr King
requires half a dozen European missionaries and at least forty
coloured teachers." The gathering together of such a staff and
its supervision required the authority of a bishop, and Copland
King was requested to accept the appointment. He refused from
a sure conviction that the work of translation to which he had
been called through Albert Maclaren was the greatest contribution
he could make. From 1897 to 1917 he produced a steady flow of
native texts, portions of Scripture, of the Prayer Book, hymns and
psalms.

The first Bishop of New Guinea, Montague John Stone-Wigg,
was enthroned at Dogura in May 1898, and in October of the
following year Copland King quietly retired two hundred and fifty
miles west along the coast and forty miles up the Mambare River.
It was the post of danger. He was on the very borders of German
New Guinea. A few months before his arrival the government

magistrate had been murdered. The natives had a reputation for hostility to the white man, and it seemed to the Governor that the Anglican Church must accept full responsibility for the area allotted her or that it must be given to another Church. Blood feuds between the natives on the Mambare were frequent. In one raid of revenge twenty-seven villagers, surprised while sleeping, were massacred. On one occasion King narrowly missed death from a tomahawk. The Mamba people knew that once over the border into German New Guinea they were safe from British law.

King went quietly on with his work of evangelization, ministering to the white gold-diggers, giving every spare minute to mastering the difficult Binandere language. The list of his publications is a formidable one. In Binandere, they include the Gospel of St Luke, the service of Holy Communion, prayers, psalms, hymns and catechism, a Binandere grammar and dictionary. These are in addition to nine translations into Wedauan, including an Old Testament lectionary of four hundred and seven pages.

In 1914 Bishop Gerald Sharp reported after a visit to the Mamba district: "In this big, far too big a district there are no fewer than 52 villages that have services held in them, and over 1,400 people attending them. Mr King is a real missionary." Three years later Copland King was forced to leave the Mamba broken in health. He died in the Coast Hospital (now Prince Henry Hospital), Sydney, on 5th October 1918. He was revising his Binandere translations until the last.

2

The Pastors

In 1898 the seven years of evangelization began to show results. The first native Christian wedding took place, the bridegroom being Selwyn, Copland King's assistant in the work of translation. On 26th July the first native Christian to be laid to rest was buried in the new cemetery at Dogura. And on the following day the first Bishop of New Guinea held his first confirmation service.

Canon Montague Stone-Wigg had been interested in the New Guinea Mission from the beginning, and one of Maclaren's last letters before leaving Cooktown in the *Grace Lynn* had been written to him. When selected as Bishop of New Guinea his responsibilities had been bluntly defined for him by a resolution of the Executive Council of the Australian Board of Missions: "That the financial responsibilities of the mission, together with the control, should be taken over by the Bishop under pledge of support from the Executive Council."

In other words, the Bishop of New Guinea was himself financially responsible for everybody and everything connected with the New Guinea Mission. So, like Albert Maclaren, Bishop Stone-Wigg spent the first months of his appointment touring Australia, preaching, lecturing, being interviewed, collecting money and trying to enlist staff. Some churchmen promised to guarantee an episcopal income of £450 per annum for five years, but the Bishop used none of it for his own purposes, spending instead much of his private income on the work of the mission.

From the time of his arrival he took his share of station work, setting out with the native "boys" at daylight to the tasks of wood-cutting or gardening, instructing the "upper mathematical" class at school in the afternoon. He particularly enjoyed the efforts of the small person nicknamed "The Archbishop" who practised a form of marginal notation. Against an indistinct figure "The Archbishop" would write *Turau, wei naeni* —"This, O my friend, is a 9." Against another problem would be written *Turau, wei a terei boai* — "O friend of mine, I have done this wrong." The Governor of Papua, after his visit of inspection, reported of the forty children: "Writing and arithmetic appeared to be up to the level of European children of the age in the case of the younger ones. The reading was very fair, all things considered."

The Bishop's primary care was to become acquainted with the work in the neighbouring villages. Taupota was suffering from the visits of unscrupulous white men seeking carriers and workers. Some natives had been murdered. The people regarded the Anglican Mission as a rallying point and were earnest in their support. In December 1898 the Bishop dedicated the church at Taupota and baptized the first group of catechumens, thirteen adults and three children.

A hurricane struck the north-east coast of Papua. The stream where the baptisms took place became a raging torrent, trees were uprooted and houses blown away. The Bishop returned to Dogura to find two whaleboats dashed to pieces, and the mission's schooner, the *Albert Maclaren*, thrown up on the beach, her main-mast smashed. He was forced to make a special appeal for £600 to repair the damage done by the hurricane.

His vision was to occupy the whole coastline that had been allotted to the Church of England. The year 1899 was a year of much building of churches, schoolrooms and houses.

At Mukawa, on the top of a cliff near Cape Vogel, were some villages. The natives were refugees from their enemies in Collingwood Bay. The position gave them the advantage of being able to throw heavy stones on the heads of their attackers. They themselves were notorious wife-beaters and practisers of infanticide. It was considered that the place was suitable for a mission station, and, with the Bishop's approval, and with tremendous efforts, a road was blasted with dynamite from the beach and a European house built on top of the cliff. There, the Bishop dreamt, might one day be a college training young Papuans for service with the mission.

The builder was Samuel Tomlinson who with his wife Elizabeth had held the position at Dogura when Maclaren had died and Copland King was sick in Sydney. As priest he was to occupy the house for nearly forty years. Near the beach at Mukawa stands a ten-foot white cross, on which is carved, "In Memory, Samuel Tomlinson, Papua, 1891–1937." And in the native language, "Our priest, the first one; peace I brought you." The words are given added significance by the inscription on a panel at the north end of the altar in the nearby church: "Adjacent to this place is the Sirage Kapukapuna, where in days past the blood of human victims was shed for the preparation of cannibal feasts. Now the Blood of the Divine Victim, once shed on Calvary, is offered for men's salvation. *Laus Deo*."

Mukawa was on the track of ships passing along the coast, and Bishop Stone-Wigg had the happy thought to erect a lighthouse, which proved a great comfort to shipping — when the mission's finances permitted it to be lit regularly. Mission stations were set up at Sinapa, Uiaku, and Wanigela, all on Collingwood Bay.

The Bishop then went south to raise funds, more particularly for the Church school he wished to establish at Samarai. The Boer War was in progress and within a few weeks £50,000 was raised for sending Australian troops to South Africa. By making innumerable speeches and constant travelling, at his own expense, Stone-Wigg was able to collect £600 in six months for the mission for which the Church in Australia held him personally responsible.

The Lieutenant-Governor of Papua, Sir George Le Hunte, about the same time expressed the official opinion: "The government owed everything to missions. The missions saved the contributing colonies thousands of pounds every year. Every penny spent by the missionaries was a help to the Queen's government. The missionaries rendered it unnecessary for the whites to move about with armed forces. They enabled their officials to leave their rifles on the ship and go inland with their umbrellas. The mission brought peace, law and order."

By 1901 the Bishop was conducting four large confirmations, the candidates coming to live at Dogura for some weeks to attend preparation classes. By the end of 1901, as the result of a decade of teaching, the number of Papuan communicants had been raised to one hundred.

At Taupota, two children, twins, were rescued from being

buried alive by their mother and were adopted by the mission. The government formed the practice of handing over to the mission "mandated" children, those cast away by their parents, and within a short time these numbered fifty-seven. The Bishop decided to "draw" the whole coast and sailed from Samarai to Basilaki Island, and round Milne Bay to East Cape. He returned with fourteen children, the half-castes of Portuguese, Malays, Japanese and Chinese. Says the Annual Report for 1907: "It is difficult to realize that their fathers hailed from such far-distant countries as Africa, Java, England, Samoa, Mauritius, Solomon Islands and other places. The dialects which the New Guinea mothers speak are many and diverse, so philologically the band of children is decidedly interesting. But it is intended that English is to be spoken." Always, within the area allotted to it, the Anglican Mission has set its face against the use of Pidgin and Motu.

There was a staff of forty-five and a hundred buildings to maintain on an income of three to four thousand pounds. The white missionaries received board and lodging to the value of 10s. a week and a quarterly allowance of £5 for personal expenses. Always the mission was in debt. The five years for which an episcopal income was guaranteed had elapsed. The Bishop's health was suffering, as a result of exposure, malaria, bronchitis and asthma. In desperation he went to England to seek sufficient money to endow the future of the diocese. He secured £5,500, which he invested. He made a note during his travels: "I preached and spoke thirteen times in the eight days covered by two Sundays and the week-days in between. In the same way on my return, landing in Fremantle on April 2, I spoke fifty-one times before I left Townsville on May 20." In all he raised £11,000 and received from a generous donor the steam launch for which he had been long asking.

By 1908, when the report of the doctors was that Stone-Wigg could no longer live in the tropics, the Bishop-Treasurer was able to report that the New Guinea Mission staff at 19 stations totalled 77, of whom 22 were British, 35 South Sea islanders, and 20 Papuan Christians. There were nearly 600 communicants, and 1,400 children attended the mission schools.

Some time after Gerald Sharp became second Bishop of New

Guinea, he was talking in Wedauan to two or three native boys at Wanigela. Two others standing behind the Bishop whispered together in their own dialect, and the priest-in-charge turned sharply to reprove them.

"Why did you speak to those boys like that?" the Bishop later protested.

"Well, my Lord, if you must know," the priest reluctantly informed him, "those two boys were sizing you up joint by joint."

Gerald Sharp was a big man, both physically and in character. He had been a fellow curate at Hammersmith with Montague Stone-Wigg, but in 1898 had not felt able to yield to the first Bishop's persuasions to go to New Guinea. A simple, lovable man himself, Gerald Sharp would quote with approval: "How is the best missionary work in all countries being done? By the simplest truths of the Gospel being stated in the simplest way in the simplest language by simple men."

In the eleven years during which he was Bishop of New Guinea, from 1910 to 1921, he saw immense changes. There was the seizure of German New Guinea, to be administered by Australia under the League of Nations as the Mandated Territory of New Guinea. There was the more intensive opening-up of rich lands to white settlers. Conditions of missionary work changed. No longer was it possible to rely so much upon South Sea islanders as teacher-evangelists; but the patient years of instruction had produced an increasing number of Papuans in their place. The lay-readers were noted for their regularity and the long distances they travelled each Sunday to conduct services. The Bishop had discovered that: "New Guinea people love not the voice of strangers as they love the voice of those who are more nearly their own people." Of great significance then was the ordination of the first Papuan priests, Peter Rautamara in December 1917, and Edwin Nuagoro the following year. In 1917 Bishop Feetham of North Queensland saw one of those impressive baptismal services which are the record of the Church's victories in Papua. At Wanigela two priests with their attendants stood nearly waist-deep in the stream:

After being signed with the cross the catechumens passed on and slowly made the passage of the stream — fifty yards wide at its mouth and flowing fast from recent heavy rains, its broad bosom marked with swirls and eddies. It is not quite strong enough to carry them off their feet, though some preferred to walk out towards the bar, where its force slackened. The adults were breast deep, and the smaller candidates were in up to the shoulders, and all came over slowly through the sweeping volume of water to our landing. Four, five, and even six were sometimes strung out between our shore and the place where baptisms were proceeding. There was something very impressive about this little procession, continuing as it did, with its personnel always renewed, for about an hour.

During his long episcopacy Bishop Sharp's "episcopal palace" consisted of a three-roomed house of coconut leaves, palm wood and bamboo, with a veranda all round it and a corrugated iron roof to catch rainwater. In 1920 he went abroad to attend the Lambeth Conference. He injured his leg and blood poisoning set in. Medical advice was that he should not return to the tropics. Translated to Brisbane as Archbishop and Metropolitan he kept a keen interest in his former diocese until his death in 1933.

When Bishop Stone-Wigg was desperately seeking men in 1899, the first priest to offer for New Guinea was Henry Newton. The missionary who had gone to open up the work along the dangerous Mambare had been brought back ill to Dogura. Newton was willing to take his place, but Copland King, who was in charge, made the decision that he would go himself, leaving the young Henry Newton in charge of Dogura. Mamba was the more difficult post, Newton might be more in line with the Church tradition of the new bishop; but there is also the possibility that King saw in Newton a future leader of the diocese.

At Dogura, Newton turned himself immediately to the work of preparing candidates for confirmation. The candidates came to live at the mission station for weeks beforehand to attend the preparation classes, which he held twice a day. In 1901, as a result of Newton's work, Bishop Stone-Wigg had been able to hold four confirmation services. The following year heavy rains and storms did so much damage to the vegetable gardens that the district was on the verge of famine. Newton took the schooner *Albert Maclaren* to Cooktown where, arriving on a Sunday evening, he preached in the Cooktown church, shipped nine tons of rice on the Monday morning and left the same day for New Guinea.

By 1904 he was opening a training college near Dogura for the preparation of native teachers and teacher-evangelists. He was parish priest for Wedau and Wamira and the other villages in Bartle Bay and in the hills behind Dogura. There was the over-sight of the large school for boys from all over the diocese, the half-caste orphanage at Ganuganuana, and the boarding-school for girls supervised by his wife. There by 1910 Mrs Newton generally had "a handful of babies playing about all over the veranda — poor little waifs and starvelings she has gathered in and nursed back to health and strength, or orphans whom, on behalf of the mission, she has adopted altogether."

But the dominant tone of Newton's life at Dogura was teaching. A fellow missionary wrote of it:

You are awakened before it is light by the bell for morning prayers; and presently after, almost before you can yawn and creep out of your mosquito net, you hear him at it — Newton, I mean, with his two theological students, Edwin and Peter — hammering away with them for a solid hour at something or other that bears upon their possible ordination some day. Very soon after breakfast the big school begins, and for half an hour (or more) he is working away with those boys and girls, drumming it into them again and again, English and Wedauan simultaneously, or indifferently, and all with such vigour that inattention is simply impossible. And then he has Edwin and Peter again for the rest of the morning in his room; and at midday he bolts up to Ganuganuana for the religious instruction in the school there. He hardly ever waits for a second cup of tea at four o'clock, for every day there is a preparation class in Chapel for those who are presently to be baptized. Whether any man, even a mission-ary priest, in such a responsible charge as that of Dogura has any right to go on, as this man does, is an open question, but it doesn't seem to harm him, and he always seems to be at leisure.

Newton did go on in this way for sixteen years until 1915 when he was chosen to succeed Bishop Gilbert White in charge of the neighbouring Diocese of Carpentaria; but in January 1922 he was back again as Bishop of New Guinea. The enthronement was very much a reunion service with Papuans attending from Ambasi, Emo, Wanigela, Mukawa, Menapi, Gayoanaki, Uga, Boianai, Nauguvara, Dogura, Doubina, Wedau, Wamira, Taupota and Awaiama. And when the Bishop celebrated at holy communion, the epistoler and gospeller were the two Papuan priests he had prepared for ordination, Edwin Nuagoro and Peter Rautomara.

If Bishop Sharp had to face the problems of the First World War and intensified white exploitation, Bishop Newton had to meet the effects of the economic depression. The grant from the Australian Board of Missions was reduced from £12,000 to £8,400, though this was partly offset by help from England. The mission's plans to extend its work into the mountains were not affected. From Menapi, the Reverend John Hunt, a veteran missionary, made his famous evangelistic tours to get into touch with the mountain people. At the inland post of Sangara, twenty-seven miles from the coast, Mr Henry Holland was supported by a staff of a nurse, a teacher and two Papuans. The chief obstacle was transport. Gona, now the chief station in the northern area, was cut off from Sangara by a swamp, and stores from Sangara had to be carried from Buna, requiring the enlistment of thirty to forty carriers each month. If only a road could be built from Gona, thought the Bishop. A way was discovered through the swamp and in 1930 the Bishop walked from Gona to Sangara inspecting the culverts and bridges under construction. He skinned both heels (he was now a man of sixty-three) and had to walk barefoot, the latter part in the dark with a hurricane lamp.

"Coming back," he wrote, "we got to a creek about 8.30 a.m., to find it in flood, so the boys could not cross. We sat down and waited two hours, not for the tide to go by, but for the current to carry off some of the floodwaters; then we could cross, carried on the boys' shoulders, just above the water, lying perfectly horizontal. Nice chance for a photo fiend, but none was there!"

An emphasis was being placed upon the medical work of the mission. At Gona the first doctor was stationed, but the burden of medical and surgical care, the relief of suffering, the care of motherless infants, the attention to the injured, were still being carried out at Dogura, Taupota, Menapi, Wanigela and Sangara by the nurses: Nurse Waldron, Nurse Townson, Nurse Kent, Nurse Mills, Nurse Brenchley. The mission was being modernized. Its steam launch, the *Maclaren King*, which could do the work of three of the earlier schooners, was maintaining a regular monthly service along the coast. At Dogura the Reverend A. H. Lambton was responsible for the construction of a dam far enough up the creek to ensure that the water would rise when conducted through a three-inch pipe across plains and hillocks up to the plateau of Dogura. The simple engineering principle involved was regarded suspiciously by the people. "Water will never walk uphill," they said. But it did.

Not less revolutionary was the building of the first permanent church at Boianai. The Reverend C. W. Light, priest-in-charge at Boianai, had seen the concrete churches at Moa Island, and Thursday Island. If the Torres Strait islanders could erect such buildings, why should not the Papuans? The native churches were beautiful but insubstantial and impermanent. Mr Light had no experience of building, but he was willing to acquire it. The church was to take five years to complete. A few experienced workers were engaged as foremen and paid from the small sum available. The others formed teams and gave their labour for periods of time while their fellow villagers looked after their gardens and provided them with food.

The builders dived for coral and burnt it, carrying the lime on their backs for half a mile to the site of the church. They carried up the shingle for the concrete from the beach, and since there was no suitable white sand near Boianai, they went twice a month in the whaleboat to an island sixteen miles away. There they filled bags of sand, some to be brought back in the whaleboat, some to be ready for the *Maclaren King* to bring across on her trips down the coast. In this way they collected seven tons of sand a month. All the timber had to be carried about five miles from the scrub to the site. The boys cut with pit saws timber for the casing of the concrete, for the building and the doors. Occasionally they had to pull down part of the walls because of a fault. The foundations, six feet deep, were filled with stone and cement. The walls were two feet thick, with buttresses fifteen feet apart.

When the Church of All Saints, Boianai, was consecrated, the Bishop was attended by seven white priests and six Papuan priests, with three Papuan deacons. There was a congregation of fifteen hundred inside and outside the church and seven hundred and fifty communicants.

In January 1936 Bishop Henry Newton was seventy years of age. He had been a missionary in the tropics, in New Guinea and Carpentaria, for thirty-seven years. He tendered his resignation, and for the next ten years he lived at Dogura as he had begun, quietly teaching the ordinands, though broken in health. On 26th

September 1947 his body was laid to rest behind the High Altar of Dogura Cathedral.

On St Paul's Day 1937 Bishop Philip Nigel Warrington Strong was enthroned at Dogura Cathedral. He was to be Bishop of the diocese for twenty-six years, more than one-third of the Church's present existence in New Guinea, and a considerable part of the following story is to a large degree a tribute to his episcopate.

3

The Years Before....

PAPUA in the quiet years before the Second World War still had a spell of enchantment hanging over it. A scent of "wildness" exuded from the green jungle over the grey beaches. It wafted out to meet the traveller as he stepped ashore from the dinghy, leaving behind him the boat smells of petrol, bilge and cargo. It was a smell composed of a thousand smells, some sweet and hauntingly elusive, some sharp and pungent, others harsh and disturbing, yet all blended into something real though indefinable, strange but always alluring. The scent came up from the moist, leaf-padded ground; it sifted down through the dense foliage of trees and hanging vines; it drifted over the wood-smoke from the village fires, enfolding one and drawing one into its very self.

Whether you were gliding off shore in a poled canoe through a glassy sea reflecting the tranquillity of dawn, or the glory of sunset; whether you were paddling silently through the moist stillness of the bush on the one-man tracks that were the chief lines of communication before wheels came, or sitting quietly on a veranda watching the moon rise over the sea while children played or sang gaily on the beach, you felt the magic of a land of mystery and infinite beauty.

Under the influence of government and missions, Papuans had surrendered most of their savagery and hostility, while still retaining their own primitive charm and manner of living. In the main their contact with Europeans had evoked admiration and trust. The men who came into their lives, both government and mission, were dedicated people whose intent was to help and teach the native people, to bring them the benefits of learning and civilization. There were, of course, the traders, recruiters, miners, seafaring men, plantation owners, with different objectives; but the Papuan soon sorted these out and recognized their worth. On the whole there was a respect for the white man, a willingness to learn from him, while reserving the right to live one's own life in one's own way.

Village life went on in its centuries-old way, except that tribal fightings and some of the bad customs were now forbidden by law. Contact with Europeans was through the government stations, from which patrols went regularly to all the main villages. The mission station formed a focal point with its church, school and dispensary. The trade stores were places where garden food could be bartered for tobacco, rice, meat and other commodities, or could be bought when one had money from sale of copra or from wages earned by "signing on", or working on the boats that plied up and down the coast.

"Signing on" was the term used for the indenture system, the method of obtaining labour for working plantations, mines, pearling boats, wharf labour, for working as store-hands, cooks, launderers, house-boys, clerks, office boys, interpreters and, later, as telephone and radio operators. The men signed on for a period of two or three years, a contract binding on both the employer and the labourer. The contract was made before a government labour officer and was only to be rescinded in the same manner. During the period of employment the "boys" were fed, housed, and clothed, given tobacco, taken care of medically, and then paid the full sum of their wages on leaving. A good part of this was spent in buying such things as knives, calicoes and fish-lines from the recruiter-trader who was bound to return them to their own villages; part of it paid tax money for the man himself and men relatives, and what was left was spent in the trade store or buried in a tin as a secret hoard.

This system in its way had some of the educational value of normal schooling, for it brought the men into close contact with Europeans, where they could watch their ways — both good and bad — and learn their language, observe rules of hygiene and see the benefit of medical treatment, learn to handle tools, a boat, an engine, learn a trade, how to cook, and get a fair idea of what European life was like. With discrimination, they could choose what they wished to learn of white men's ways, and blend it with the best of their own and so improve life in their villages when they returned.

In another category were the men who joined the Papuan Constabulary. These were government staff, and usually retained their positions for many years, attached to the government stations scattered throughout the territory. Some were specially selected and trained to handle arms, and to know how to use them in emergency. These formed a unit known as the Armed Constabulary, and much fine work was done by them in penetrating new country alongside their white officers and in bringing it under control.

Before the Second World War, Papua and the Territory of New Guinea were under two separate administrations, Papua being under the charge of Lieutenant-Governor Sir John Hubert Murray from 1908 to 1940, and the mandated territory being under an Administrator. There was little contact between the two territories, the residents of each adopting a rather superior attitude towards those of the other. In the mandated territory the German system of government had been rigid towards the native peoples. The men workers were known as "bois", the women as "meris", and the small, runabout boys as "mankis", and all were regarded as inferior beings and treated accordingly.

Papuan administration, under Sir Hubert Murray, adopted a less discriminatory attitude, and the laws forbade ill-treatment of native people. Self-righteous looks from *this* side of the border were cast at the "other territory", and looks from there beamed pity and contempt for weakness and soft laws in molly-coddling the natives.

Lae, Salamaua and Madang were the chief ports on the north coast of New Guinea and Wau and Bulolo the only inland towns, just budding round the gold holdings. Samarai, with its land-locked harbour, was the shipping and shopping centre for the islands at the eastern end of Papua and for the plantations and mission stations on the coast. Cargo and passengers were off-loaded there, and schooners and launches waiting in port would soon be loaded and on their way to their far-off destinations. The three main stores on the island would have their stocks replenished to tide them over for the next six weeks, the bustle of the ship's

Canon James Benson, priest-in-charge at Gona when Japanese soldiers landed in July 1942.

John Duffill, mission builder at Isivita, martyred August 1942.

The Cathedral of St Peter and St Paul, Dogura.

An ordination service in the Cathedral of St Peter and St Paul, Dogura.

departure would die down, and Samarai would slip back into its dreamy idyllic existence.

The Anglican Mission boat, for years under the Reverend A. J. Thompson's careful supervision, would have the stores for all the mission stations up the coast methodically loaded, so that those for the nearer stations were on top, and the farther ones at the bottom. Passengers would embark; meals for the journey were amply provided for. Father and mother might be there to wave good-bye to young missionaries, and the *Maclaren King* would set off yet once again on its voyage through the green-wooded islands, round the point, across Milne Bay, through the beautiful but treacherous little passage at East Cape, and along the lovely coastline to Dogura, or farther.

Dogura, the headquarters of the mission, was a place where inspiration uplifted the soul and prepared it for the special consecration that missionary work in Papua demanded. In October 1939, a few weeks after the beginning of the war in Europe, the great Cathedral of St Peter and St Paul was consecrated. Built of reinforced concrete in the Norman style, with massive pillars and round arches, it gave an impression of lasting, natural strength. The building and consecration were the crowning achievements of the work of previous decades. Papuan Christians, a hundred and seventy men altogther, from all the different areas of the Anglican Mission in Papua, had each voluntarily given their labour for at least three months to the construction, which was under the supervision of one white man, the Reverend Robert Jones. The cathedral is 170 feet long and broad in proportion. The actual cost was only £4,000, though in Australia it would have been many times that sum. Of the 3,000 natives who came from all parts of Papua for its consecration, over 1,500 received communion on that day. The following morning there were 800 communicants at the sung eucharist at 7 a.m., and Bishop Strong recorded that it was "an inspiring thing to see Papuan Christians of all ages, representative of different tribes and districts from right up to the north of the diocese, down to Wedau and Taupota, some of whom in the past would have been at enmity with one another, now kneeling before the altar to unite themselves with the Lord, who has brought them to realize that they are all brethren in the one family of God". In memory of the early missionaries, stained-glass windows and furnishings

C

had been donated from Australia, gifts that had been the result of the efforts of church and youth organizations all over the Commonwealth.

Dogura, steeped in the history of the Anglican Mission, was the preliminary training-ground for most of the young missionaries. There the woman medical missionary received an introduction to the problems she would have to face on an isolated station. It was a gigantic task to break through the barrier of fear and fatalism that had been an integral part of every Papuan mind for centuries past. Victory was achieved by a life preserved here, a healing there, a relief from pain following treatment, healing of gaping yaws, ulcers after injections, and an apparently lifeless baby given breath. The medical missionary had to build up confidence among the Papuan women, a confidence based on personal friendship; she endeavoured to bring to them a realization of their individual importance as human souls. Cerebral malaria would mean the visit of a mother carrying a baby, inert and in a coma, or screaming shrilly in delirium. The nurse would have to put everything aside and give all attention to the small babe: tepid baths, quinine, and a sedative would be given every chance to do their work, while a bed was prepared and fluids made ready for the child's return to consciousness. If treatment was effective, one breathed a sigh of relief and a prayer of thanksgiving, but if all proved to be of no avail, one handed the quiet little body back into the arms of the wailing mother, sharing her heartbreak, but unable to plumb the depths of her pagan misery and despair.

In the night might come a sharp rat-tat on the steps and a low murmur of voices. At the door would be a man, with a companion holding a lamp or firestick. "Please, Sister, you come quick! Grace Mary big sick, she can't take baby!" Questioning would bring to light the fact that "Grace Mary" had been in labour for two days and was having trouble in getting her baby born.

At an inland mission station such as Sangara a couple of mission-boys would be trained to do casual dressings and the "daily dabs" for the schoolchildren in the mornings, and in the afternoons they would wash bandages and clean up the dispensary after school. They also accompanied Sister on her visits to the villages helping to carry things and to interpret the conversations, thus learning quite a considerable amount in a roundabout way. The lonely missionary Sister would sometimes have to escort a sick patient to a station where there was a doctor, to see that the litter was carried carefully and to attend to the patient on the way. The visit to Dogura for conference was the great event of the year. Ahead would be the excitement of meeting fellow missionaries who had not been seen for a year or more. There was the long journey down the coast on the *Maclaren King* to Dogura, with the overnight stops at other mission stations, putting up stretchers and mosquito nets for the night, the babble of talk and laughter around the meal table, the ever increasing number on the boat as it picked up fresh members of the staff at each stop. Then, finally, came the gathering at Dogura with its serious discussions and decisions, its lighter moments of entertainment, and deeper joy of communal worship and devotion.

Quickly the time went, and, on the return trip, regretful farewells were made at each stopping-place as staff disembarked at their stations, until at Gona only the lone member from the Mamba station remained. In 1941, many of these farewells were made for the last time.

4

The Coming of War

EUROPE had been at war for two years before the outbreak in the Pacific with the attack on Pearl Harbour by the Japanese. During those two years the people of Papua felt something of the conflict. For the first time troops were stationed in Papua — it had been the proud boast of Sir William MacGregor that he had never had to call for military assistance. The war troubled the minds of the Papuan people. White men had taught them not to fight, and now the same white men were fighting with other men. Still they realized that their own homes and lands had been protected for them by the government from the unscrupulous people who would have taken them away had they been able to do so. Across the world, they were told, Britain had entered into war with Germany to prevent their taking away the homes and lands of the Polish and other peoples of Europe. Many of the young men joined the Papuan Infantry Battalion and others gave their spare time to local defence forces.

The Japanese attack on the American Naval Base at Pearl Harbour took place on 7th December 1941. It marked the beginning of a movement towards the south from Japan aimed at conquering the entire Pacific region. On 11th December they occupied Guam and so began the battle for the Philippines. They attacked British North Borneo and landed in Sarawak on 17th December. On the same day the order was given for the evacuation of all white women from Papua and New Guinea. Hong Kong capitulated on Christmas Day. On 2nd January 1942 the war came to New Guinea with the bombing of Rabaul, which was bombed again, only much more heavily, on the 20th. Between the 21st and 24th, Lae, Salamaua and Bulolo were bombed, and Lae and Salamaua were abandoned. On the 22nd Japanese ships were seen approaching Rabaul, and the civilian population was evacuated into the jungle. On the following day Rabaul was occupied by the Japanese. A few days later all men in Papua and New Guinea under forty-five years of age were called up for military service.

Realizing that Samarai would almost certainly be a target for the Japanese, Bishop Strong made arrangements to transfer as much of the mission equipment as possible from there to Dogura. The tiny *Maclaren King*, aided by another boat, each doing more than one trip, succeeded in moving much of the Samarai property, together with supplies of such essentials as meat, flour, tea, sugar and trade tobacco. The last load left Samarai on Friday, 30th January. On the following day a Japanese plane flew over Samarai, the first to be seen there.

On that same Saturday, Bishop Strong, in a radio message to the mission staff, told of the move from Samarai to Dogura and went on to say:

Now I would like a heart-to-heart talk with you. As far as I know, you are all at your posts and I am very glad and thankful about this. I have from the first felt that we must endeavour to carry on our work in all circumstances no matter what the cost may ultimately be to any of us individually. God expects this of us. The Church at home, which sent us out, will surely expect it of us. The Universal Church expects it. The tradition and history of missions requires it of us. Missionaries who have been faithful to the uttermost and are now at rest are surely expecting it of us. The people whom we serve expect it of us. We could never hold up our faces again, if, for our own safety, we all forsook Him and fled when the shadows of the Passion began to gather around Him in His Spiritual Body, the Church in Papua. Our life in the future would be burdened with shame and we could not come back here and face our people again; and we would be conscious always of rejected opportunities. The history of the Church tells us that missionaries do not think of themselves in the hour of danger and crisis, but of the Master who called them to give their all, and of the people they have been trusted to serve and love to the uttermost. His watchword is none the less true today, as it was when he gave it to the first disciples — "Whosoever will save his life will lose it, and whosoever will lose his life for My sake and the Gospel's shall find it."

No one requires us to leave. No one has required us to leave. The reports some of you have heard of orders to this effect did not emanate from official or authoritative sources. But even if anyone had required us to leave, we should then have had to obey God rather than men. We could not leave unless God, who called us, required it of us, and our spiritual instinct tells us He would never require such a thing at such an hour.

Our people need us now more than ever before in the whole history of the mission. To give but two examples:

1. *Our Native Ministry.* We have accepted a big responsibility in the eyes of all Christendom in founding a native ministry. We have given birth to it. We are responsible before God and the Church for its growth and development on sound Catholic lines. It is still but in its infancy. We cannot leave it to sink back into heathenism. We must stand by that to which we have given birth.

2. *Our Papuan Women.* Our influence is just beginning to tell with them. How would they fare if all our women missionaries left? It would take years to recover what the locusts had eaten. Our Papuan women need the influence of women missionaries today more than ever.

No, my brothers and sisters, fellow workers in Christ, whatever others may do, we cannot leave. We shall not leave. We shall stand by our trust. We shall stand by our vocation.

We do not know what it may mean to us. Many think us fools and mad. What does that matter? If we are fools, "we are fools for Christ's sake". I cannot foretell the future. I cannot guarantee that all will be well — that we shall all come through unscathed. One thing only I can guarantee is that if we do not forsake Christ here in Papua in His Body, the Church, He will not forsake us. He will uphold us; He will strengthen us and He will guide us and keep us through the days that lie ahead. If we all left, it would take years for the Church to recover from our betrayal of our trust. If we remain — and even if the worst came to the worst and we were all to perish in remaining — the Church will not perish, for there would have been no breach of trust in its walls, but its foundations and structure would have received added strength for the future building by our faithfulness unto death.

This, I believe, is the resolution of you all. Indeed, I have been deeply moved and cheered more than I can say by letters I have received from many of our staff this week who have been in a position to communicate with me, and I have reason to believe that others who have not had that opportunity think and feel the same way. Our staff, I believe, stands as a solid phalanx in this time of uncertainty. Their influence has already had a stabilizing effect on the community, and though harm has already been done, counsels of sanity are beginning to prevail again in the territory before the damage has become irretrievable. However, let us not judge others, but let us only follow duty as we see it. If we are a solid phalanx, let us see to it in the days to come that it is a phalanx of Divine Grace, for only so can it remain unshaken.

I know there are special circumstances which may make it imperative for one or two to go (if arrangements can be made for them to do so). For the rest of us, we have made our resolution to stay. Let us not shrink from it. Let us not go back on it. Let us trust and not be afraid.

To you all I send my blessing. The Lord be with you.

On 3rd February Port Moresby was raided, and for the first time the war had affected Papua. Four days later Samarai, by then deserted, was bombed. Civil administration ceased on 12th February, and martial law was declared in both Papua and New Guinea. Japanese forces landed at Lae and Salamaua on 8th March 1942. Meanwhile the Bishop was travelling along the coast in the *Maclaren King* to visit every station. He wrote: "I felt it to be my duty in those early months of 1942 to visit our mission stations as often as I could that I might strive to strengthen the hands of those who were carrying on nobly at their stations and yet in such isolation and possible danger."

During his travels the Bishop came to Gona on 10th March to see Father James Benson and, having spoken to him, set off by sea southward in the direction of Buna, the chief Administration centre in the area. Some time after the Bishop had sailed, a Japanese seaplane flew low over Gona. Later a man staggered into the station from the direction of Buna and gasped out that two bombs had been dropped on Buna, that Buna was finished and that everyone had been killed.

What had been attacked was the *Maclaren King*, which had been anchored in shore not far from Buna. The two bombs had fallen in the ocean, one on either side of the vessel. The crew abandoned the ship and struck out for the shore, only to be machine-gunned by the Japanese plane after it had circled. The swimmers found safety by diving underwater. At this stage the pilot of the plane noticed the small launch containing the Bishop approaching the beach on the other side of the bay. The Bishop and Mr John Duffill and party barely had time to scramble ashore and throw themselves flat on the sand before the plane roared low overhead riddling the small boat with bullets from stem to stern. The plane then landed on the water and began to spray bullets in the direction of the launch party. Fortunately they had moved to a safer place.

By this time small guns were being fired from the shore and the Japanese, fearing that they might suffer damage to the aircraft, took off. So ended the first action against the enemy on the north-east coast of Papua. After the plane had gone, the Bishop and others knelt and thanked God for their deliverance. The *Maclaren King* left at six o'clock that evening intending to travel under cover of darkness; and the Bishop carried with him his Office Book almost shot to pieces in the encounter.

Papua was not actually invaded until 21st July 1942, when enemy forces landed at various points from Gona to Buna. A road ran through the bush from Gona and eventually linked up with the road to Kokoda from the coast. The Japanese had decided to advance along both of these roads to Kokoda, then cross the Owen Stanley Range and march into Port Moresby. The Bishop wrote: "The landing at Gona and Buna brought to a sudden end all our work in the north except at the Mamba where Archdeacon Gill was able for a time to continue. At Gona, Sangara, Isivita, and at Eroro the work was brought to a sudden cessation. The diocese was no longer a unity. The northern and southern parts of our mission area were severed one from the other. A curtain was drawn down over the north, and we in the south did not know what had befallen our fellow workers, what was becoming of our Papuan Christians."

5

The Martyrs

OF GONA

GONA when war broke out in the Pacific was a beautiful and well-cared-for mission station. Approached from the shore, it opened out to an area of park-like proportions. Trees, old and of all shapes and postures, lined the foot-track running parallel to the beach and leading through the mission station to the villages on either side. Flowering tulip and other trees were scattered across the lawns, garden beds were gay with canna and croton bushes, hibiscus flourished everywhere, gardenia, granny's bonnet and vinca (both alba and rosea) brightened odd corners with their whites, pinks and purples.

It was not easy to believe that just behind the station the land gave way to mangrove swamp consisting of thick, often prickly undergrowth, and damp slushy conditions underfoot in which bred myriads of mosquitoes including the anopheles, the carrier of malaria. Father Benson, the priest-in-charge, once wrote to a friend that he thought Gona must surely be the home of the anopheles.

The Reverend James Benson had emigrated from Yorkshire to Australia to become a lay member of a bush brotherhood. He was subsequently ordained and, after marrying, joined the staff of the New Guinea Mission. Owing to the ill-health of his wife he had returned to Australia to become a parish priest on the south coast of New South Wales. There a tragic accident took the lives of his wife and young family. He joined the Community of the Ascension, a religious community which hoped to undertake work in New Guinea. A change of plans by the Community led him to withdraw from the Order and to return to the staff of the Diocese of New Guinea in January 1937.

In December 1941 All Souls' Mission Station at Gona was in his charge, and the work of the hospital and school was supervised by Sister May Hayman and Miss Mavis Parkinson. The station consisted of a church, a hospital, a school, houses for the staff, the mission house occupied at one time by the doctor and his family, a small dispensary and workshop. The hospital, slightly back from the beach, was well constructed of sawn timber and was adequate for the needs of the district. A tidal creek spanned by a fragile bridge separated this part of the mission station (known as Kikiri) from that which contained the church and schools and the residences of the priest-in-charge, the teachers and mission-boys. This area was known as Dambuderari.

Across the Dambuderari bridge Mavis Parkinson walked each day to her schools, and at Kikiri Sister May Hayman attended to her duties in the dispensary and hospital, doing village-visiting and undertaking long patrols (known as "walkabouts") to out-stations and villages. After the departure of the doctor and his family in 1938 she also took over the housekeeping for the rest of the staff. When the Japanese landed at Gona the dinner was actually cooking, and later a Japanese officer told Father Benson they had found it to perfection.

Care of the gardens was part of Mavis Parkinson's duty as head of the schools. With her small army of schoolchildren she kept the gardens in a beautiful condition as her predecessors had done. With the everlasting fight against the ubiquitous grass-seeds, the sound of a swishing "peto", or the sight of a row of small children on their knees, was a daily one, as the heads of reddish-brown grass-seeds were swiped off by peto, or plucked by small brown fingers. Besides the routine garden-duty chores, grass-control was also a useful and fitting punishment-duty for misbehaviour, late-coming or other misdemeanours

Father Benson had great admiration for Mavis Parkinson as a teacher, saying that the examination results of the yearly inspec-tion by the Queensland District Schools' inspector were never higher than when she taught at Gona. In prewar days the govern-ment support for missions was issued on a quota basis. Five shillings was the grant for each child in a certain grade who passed the examination, and the grant was raised by 2s. 6d. or

5s. od. increasingly for each grade, with a maximum of £1 for
Grade 5 (which was practically non-existent at the time). Since
these amounts were the grant for the whole year, it can be understood how important it was that the mission had never obtained
less than the maximum for each year.

Mavis Parkinson was a Queenslander of the city of Ipswich,
where she lived with her parents and sister during her early years.
She was educated at the Ipswich Girls' Grammar School, where
she became a prefect. She attended St Paul's Church of England
and Sunday School and later taught in the Sunday school. She
was a Comrade of St George and a keen Girl Guide. One of the
St Paul's clergy said of her, "I believe she had a vision which gave
her inspiration; there was a power about her life." It was not
surprising that, though happily employed in a clerical position,
she felt herself called upon to offer for mission work. She spent a
year in one of the schools of the Sisters of the Sacred Advent to
gain teaching experience, then went to Sydney for the twelve
months' course at the Australian Board of Missions' training
college.

She was never pious or stuffy. Her fellow students recall many
stories of her gay approach to life. On one occasion the students
were unexpectedly told that they would be sitting on the Monday
morning with Methodist and New Guinea cadet students for an
anthropology examination. One student shut herself up in her
room for the week-end studying her hardest. Mavis Parkinson and
a friend went to the city and ate chocolates busily in the hope of
being too bilious to face the examination. A transport strike prevented them from arriving back at the college until very late. They
found the Warden pacing the footpath in great anxiety. She feared
that the shock of the announcement of the examination might
have caused them to do away with themselves. On the Monday
they faced the examination with the rest.

A "very important lady" came to the college to "look over"
the students. The girls were skylarking after dinner while washing
up. Mavis found herself locked in the pantry and decided to say
her evening prayers, leaning against the door. The Warden
brought the visitor to the kitchen to say good-bye. The door of the
pantry was hastily unlocked, and Mavis rolled out on the kitchen
floor. Looking up, she said indignantly to the visitor, "You
interrupted my prayers!" The "very important lady" left the

college with mixed ideas about the nature of young missionary
candidates. It was, however, the same girl who declined an offer
of marriage, acting according to her conviction, "I want to give
my life to our Lord while I am young."

Sister May Hayman joined the New Guinea Mission in 1936.
She was an Adelaide girl who had served in the Adelaide, Melbourne, Dubbo and Canberra hospitals. The influence of Archdeacon C. S. Robertson, then Rector of St John's, Canberra,
turned her thoughts to mission work. "Merry" Hayman was a
small, sprite-like person with pretty hair and very bright eyes.
She had served on the stations at Dogura and Boianai before
going to Gona. She was immensely happy in her work and shortly
before the Japanese invaded Papua announced her engagement
to the Reverend Vivian Redlich, the priest-in-charge of Sangara
mission station.

The first half of 1942 found the Anglican missionaries resolved to
stay at their posts scattered along the whole northern coast of
Papua. The Bishop's broadcast of 31st January reflected the
wishes of the mission staff. In New Britain, Rabaul fell on 23rd
January and, across the border in the Mandated Territory of New
Guinea, Lae and Salamaua were occupied by the Japanese on
8th March. In Papua, Port Moresby was being bombed nightly
and even in daylight.

On the mission stations, from Dewade near the New Guinea
border to Taupota in the far south-east, life went on in the
ordinary way. There were no longer any six-weekly trips of the
mission boats bringing stores and mail. News of the outside world
was only such as could be gleaned from the small erratic radios,
run on wet batteries, which had a habit of petering out at critical
times, or from chance visitors, patrol officers, or men from a
passing army boat. As the tempo of the war increased in New
Britain and in the mandated territory, refugees began to stream
down into Papua. Some had escaped from New Britain in small
boats or canoes, or had been picked up by navy or army boats.
Some made their way across the border from New Guinea, a
hazardous step ahead of the Japanese. Thirty refugees arrived at
Gona by canoe from Salamaua and, after spending a night at the
station, set off on the five days' walk to the Kokoda airstrip from
where they would be taken by air to Port Moresby.

The refugees who were making their way down the coast to Samarai, hoping to get shipped from there, would call at the missions, Gona, Eroro, Wanigela, Mukawa, grateful for the food and shelter for the night, hot baths and clean clothes. They told tales of dangers and hardships encountered and endured, over which the missionaries might reflect until the next party or odd stragglers arrived. These latter were usually Allied servicemen who had been forced down from the air after action with the Japanese, or had been cut off from their units in land engagements. Father Benson was able to send reassuring letters to the relatives of some of the servicemen. After leaving Gona, the refugees would give news of that northern outpost to the missionaries to the south-east as they talked over dinner.

At Gona the staff had certainly no idea that the Japanese would ever land their army of invasion at this relatively unimportant part of the coast, but they did expect that small forces might be landed with the task of forming airstrips and, of course, there was always the danger of Japanese survivors from crashed aircraft. They were also aware that the Allied bombers that passed to the north and at first seemed unopposed were now returning in smaller formations.

The crash of an American plane not far from Gona and the gathering of the survivors at the station before they left for Dogura and Milne Bay reinforced Father Benson's wish that the two women missionaries should leave the station. About thirteen miles south-east of Gona was the administrative station of Buna. This was now under the control of ANGAU, which had taken the place of the civilian government, and had incorporated into its staff all the officers of the Administration. Mr J. Atkinson, the Magistrate, and his assistant, Mr Alan Champion, who were in charge of Buna, tried several times to persuade the girls to go inland. Sister Hayman and Mavis Parkinson refused to go until they had been instructed by the Bishop. He advised the girls by radio to go to a safer area, but they declined.

Then came a series of radio warnings from Samarai to people living in part of the territory. Many were advised to come immediately to Samarai, others were told to be ready to leave at a moment's notice. At the end of the official messages the announcer said, "For you people on the north-east coast, I have no definite instructions for you, but if you don't want to leave your bones on the beaches, I think you had better clear out too."

It was not certain that the message was official and came from the military authorities. Father Benson tried to contact the Bishop, but could not do so for he was aboard the *Maclaren King* somewhere along the coast. Mavis Parkinson had not secured her parents' permission to remain at Gona, which, considering her age, the Bishop believed she should obtain. From the time of the arrival of the thirty refugees from Salamaua — "thirty bearded and sunburnt refugees from the bombed township in a dozen great canoes from the Waria River" — Father Benson had been urging that his "two Sisters"* should go from what was becoming a danger area.

From Buna came a message from Mr Atkinson saying that he accepted the wireless announcement as official. He would be leaving the following morning for Kokoda and suggested a place of rendezvous with the mission staff. Father Benson intended to stay at Gona himself, but he encouraged the Sisters to pack and disposed of most of the stores by distributing them to the mission teachers. Late in the afternoon a small launch arrived from Eroro, some seventy miles down the coast. Father Newman had come to see what the Gona staff intended to do. He did not regard the radio message as official and was staying until advised to leave by the Bishop. Both priests agreed that the women should go, and since Mrs Newman was going to Kokoda with Mr Atkinson (the tracks from Buna and Gona joined a few miles inland) it seemed a good idea that the Sisters should join the Magistrate's party.

The following morning, after an early celebration of the Holy Communion, the travellers left the station accompanied by twelve of the mission-boys — "they could have had a couple of hundred helpers had they wished". The two priests accompanied the women for the first few miles and with a feeling of considerable relief watched them heading off towards the Owen Stanley mountains.

Five days later Father Benson was amazed to see the Sisters walking back into the Gona mission compound. Mr Atkinson had taken his radio with him, and every night the party listened to the news. They learnt that the radio announcement from

---

*"Sisters" is commonly used in Papua for both medical and teaching white missionaries.

Samarai was not official and that the Bishop was staying on at
Dogura. At Sangara the Sisters found Nurse Brenchley and Lilla
Lashmar still at their posts. Over the air Mavis's plea to her
parents was heard all down the coast, "Please let me stay". The
consent was given, and she and Sister Hayman turned and walked
back to Gona. The following day, school and hospital were func-
tioning as usual.

On 7th and 8th May occurred the Battle of the Coral Sea, a
victory for the Allied forces that gave a sudden importance in
Japanese and Allied military strategy to the small mission station
at Gona. The Japanese invasion fleet had set out with orders to
destroy Allied sea and air forces, raid Townsville and cover a
landing at Port Moresby. In the Battle of the Coral Sea, which
was fought entirely in the air, the Japanese lost two aircraft carriers and the majority of planes on the third were damaged. The
convoy turned back to Rabaul. From 3rd to 6th June the Battle
of Midway Island took place, when the Japanese lost four carriers
and about two hundred and fifty planes. The Japanese military
strategy was changed, and along the road from Gona built
through the swamps by Henry Holland for Bishop Newton was
to pass a great part of the Japanese Army ordered to cross the
wild and rugged Owen Stanley Range and capture Port Moresby.

One morning in June at about eleven o'clock when the children at Gona were out playing on the deba-deba, an American
plane flew very low over the station in the direction of Buna. The
fighter plane was in pursuit of another aircraft out to sea. The
distant sound of gunfire was heard from the station, and then
two more planes came out of the clouds attacked the American
who turned from the battle and made his way back to land. His
plane was on fire and losing height rapidly. It seemed as though
the pilot was making his way to the playing-field. Whether that
was his idea and he decided against it, or whether his plane was
out of control cannot be certain, but the plane flew just beyond
the station crashing into the bush. As it passed over the end of
the station, something white fell from it. With his parachute still
unopened the pilot landed near the foot of a large tulip-tree at
the end of the church. Mavis Parkinson was the first to reach the
battered airman, and Father Benson ran to the burning plane.
It was a single-seater, and nothing could be done. The dead pilot,
Lieutenant Howard Winkler of the United States, was carried by

the Sisters into the church, and later buried in the mission cemetery.

Late in the afternoon of Tuesday, 21st July, the Gona mission staff witnessed the arrival of the first of the Japanese forces that were to engage with Australians, Americans and Papuans in the historic campaign of the Kokoda Trail. Father Benson was busy in the workshop when a boy rushed to the door, shouting, "Father! Great ships are here." Coming from the north-west was a transport escorted by four destroyers. Dazed by the shock the priest walked to his house and collected a few items, his old white cassock, Office Book, watch, a compass that had been given him by an American airman, tobacco, pencil and notebook, and a few handkerchiefs. The people of the area, who had never seen any vessel larger than the *Maclaren King*, were hurriedly making their way, with sleeping mats, clay cooking pots, little pigs and babies, along the bush tracks that led from the station, or eastward along the beach.

The priest, the two Sisters and the senior native teacher, who had sent his family away, watched the transport and destroyers work their way in shore. Any hope that the ships might be Allied vessels was dispelled when three or four planes with Allied markings attacked the convoy. The battle was a brief encounter and the planes flew away, their ammunition exhausted. Boats were lowered from the transport's sides and hundreds of men tumbled into them. A lone signaller from Buna, who was on his way to Ambasi and had had lunch at the mission, prepared calmly to meet the invasion with his tommy-gun. "No!" said the priest, "Don't! With one gun you can do nothing." They shook hands, and the signaller disappeared in the bush.

Father Benson had often jokingly said that if Japanese came he would invite their captain to tea —"It would be the only sensible thing to do"— but now he had the responsibility of the Sisters, and when shells began to land in the mission compound and a barrage of fire swept the beach-strip it was obviously impossible to remain. Collecting some food, mosquito nets and clothes, the missionaries set off by the little track at the back of the mission with three of the native boys. As they turned into the jungle the Japanese landed half a mile away to the west.

The missionaries' experiences during the next nineteen days are best described in a letter from Mavis Parkinson to her parents.

I know how terribly worried you all must be, but if thoughts can comfort, I know you must be comforted.

Fr Benson, May and I are in a little hide-out in the bush and, indeed, are doing what probably few white men have done before, living in the heart of the Papuan jungle.

On Sunday, July 18,* Sergeant Hewitt and Signaller Palmer arrived at Gona on their way through from Buna and as they had a few days to spare decided to salvage the American plane which had crashed on our station.

As we had visitors at night, May and I dressed for dinner in our long frocks, and afterwards, as it was rather warm, took the light and gramophone out under the palm-trees on the lawn where we talked and ate chocolate the boys had received in Comforts Funds Parcels.

Tuesday passed as usual (I was examining the schools) and early in the afternoon I pressed my pretty blue georgette evening frock to wear that night.

About 4.45 p.m. I heard yells from Lancelot, one of my pupil teachers: "Sister, Sister, are you there? Oh, Sister, come quickly!" as he ran up the path from the beach. I simply could not believe my eyes. There were four big ships not far out to sea, and another two on the skyline. Then the boats farther out opened fire on those nearer the beach, burst after burst of shellfire until the ground shook with the explosions. Then ensued a most thrilling naval battle, the warships, both ours and Japan's seeming to move around like tiny boats, they were so quick. Then the transports put down dinghies, and men got into them, so we decided we'd better move to a healthier spot.

We rushed up to the house, grabbed a box, and flung as much as we could into it, our nicest dresses, some undies, comb, toothbrushes, soap, shoes, etc. The soldiers had meanwhile gone up the beach. Our mission-boys were so frightened, but so brave, and carried our things for us along the only road we could take — the mission road to Kokoda.† It was by then 6.30, and as it was fairly dark we stopped at the first little garden house along the track, a mile from Gona. There we said evensong with the boys, put up our mosquito nets and prepared to settle down. About a quarter of an hour later we heard footsteps on the road, and voices. We thought they were village people going into hiding, and I called out to them first in English, "Boys, come here, we want you", then the same in Motu, but only silence answered. Soon another lot came, and again we called out, and Father whistled, but again silence. Then we saw a torch flash,

---

*19th July. The account of the engagement with the Allied aircraft is obviously confused and inaccurate.
†The road from Gona.

D

heard a clank of a bayonet, and knew we had been calling out to patrols of Japanese soldiers passing up the mission road. Our way to Isivita or Sangara was cut off, and we could hear the Japs all around us on the various Kokoda roads. May and I thought we'd like a run for our money, so suggested that we should wait our chance of getting over the Kokoda road and into the other bush on the other side. We grabbed up our mosquito nets, groundsheets, a blanket each, a tin of biscuits, and a parcel of chocolate Mr Champion had sent us the day before, a billy can for water, and Father had his walkabout haversack.

We left everything else, and crept down the path to the track where the Japs were, and as soon as the way was clear, between patrols, we went for our lives across that road and into the thick wet grass on the other side. We pushed through the undergrowth to a log, a damp rotten one, where we spent the rest of the night.

We were glad to see dawn, and after eating a biscuit each pushed on through the bush. By a great mercy Father had a compass in his bag, one given us by Lieutenant Dickenson, an American pilot who had crashed near us and stayed at Gona for some weeks. We'd not gone far when the first raid on Gona occurred. We crouched under a big tree, hoping to get some protection. The air seemed thick with bombs and shells, the planes roared just over our heads, and the air seemed full of dog-fights.

Things quietened down after eight or ten minutes, and we said mattins, then continued our journey through the bush. Less than every half-hour throughout that day there was a raid. We had lunch (two milk coffee biscuits and a piece of chocolate each), and again pushed on, but about 3.30 p.m. we came to a big tree with a brush turkey's nest at its foot, and we decided to make our camp for the night. There had already been 19 raids on Gona* that day (surely a record) and as soon as the moon rose they started again. Next day, to our dismay, we got into a sago swamp, and only if you'd been in this country could you know what that means — prickly, almost impenetrable undergrowth, slushy mud underfoot, into which it is possible to sink up to one's waist and even neck, and always the chance of crocodiles. However, we decided to go east, retracing our footsteps, and try to get around that way. Soon we came to a clean running stream, and while Father went farther up the river, May and I stripped and got into the water. Oh, it was heavenly to feel the cool water on our bodies, and to bathe our poor legs, torn by the prickles and thorns of the bush. Then we went on for some distance until,

*By Allied aircraft. General MacArthur had planned to form a base at Buna, but the Japanese landed first.

to our great joy, we came to natives. They made a great fuss of us and prepared food for us. My word, we were pretty hungry too, and just ate taro and sweet potato out of the cooking pot — no salt or anything! They told us of Japs on the tracks near by — more patrols, of course, and also told us we were on the track to Siai, our out-station.

We walked hard the next morning, and about lunch-time met three Bakumbari (a village about ten miles from Gona) boys on the track. We were quite overwhelmed by their affectionate greetings. They carried our swags then, and on we went, and arrived at Sageri about mid-afternoon. From there we sent a letter on to Siai, telling Father John Yariri, our assistant native priest, who happened to be at Siai giving the Christians their communion, to meet us the next day. Next morning off we went again, the Sageri people carrying our swags, and just beyond Orosusu met Father John, Nathaniel (the Siai teacher) and a crowd of Siai people, Christian and heathen. As long as I live I shall never forget the welcome they gave us. They hugged us and patted us for ages, and actually cried over us.

They took us on to Siai station and there we had another demonstration, by the women this time. They brought us food and hot water for a bath. May and I took off our filthy dresses and washed them, and while they dried, May wore a cassock of Father John's and I wore an alb!

The people decided the best thing to do would be to build us a cottage in the bush where we should be hidden until things cleared up a little. We could still hear the bombs falling on Gona. So we came to this house just a fortnight today (August 10th).* Mr Chester sent May and me some clothes belonging to a woman who had evacuated in January — dresses and scanties, and a few towels and two nightdresses, so we are beautifully fitted out.

We've simply no idea what is happening, though we do know that the bombing of Gona has stopped. Of course we hear all sorts of rumours. We heard of fighting for Kokoda at Olive Hill,† and now we hear of fighting on the Moresby road. We heard that the Japs' cartridges are finished and the fighting is now hand to hand.

Whenever the missionaries visited the village of Siai they heard rumours of the Japanese coming nearer. Father Benson thought he should try to get in touch with Father Romney Gill in the Mamba district, but the villagers had become too frightened to

*The date appears inaccurate.
†Probably Oive Ridge.

move away from their own part of the country. They were three days' walk from the Mamba and the priest believed that the Japanese could have no military objective there. His concern for the two women increased when he was told that an old sorcerer at Oitanandi had said it would be better to kill the Europeans, otherwise the Japanese would punish everyone. The same man threatened to come and kill the missionaries himself. A young catechumen from Oitanandi promised to keep an eye on the sorcerer, but that night the priest slept very little.

On 8th August Father Benson decided that they would have to move and head towards the Mamba district, but late that afternoon two Australian soldiers walked into the camp. They said they belonged to a party of three other Australians, five American airmen and five men from the Papuan Infantry Battalion. They had all been hiding and had decided to work towards the east, cross the Japanese lines along the Kokoda road, cross the Owen Stanleys behind Cape Nelson (where the mountains were lower), and make their way to Rigo on the southern coast and from there to Port Moresby. Hearing of the presence of the missionaries, the two soldiers had come to invite them to join the party.

The Sisters were in favour of joining the soldiers. Father Benson reminded them that the journey would take six to eight weeks, that the number of men who had walked across Papua was less than a dozen, and that these were members of well-equipped expeditions. The missionaries' boots were already bound to their feet by strips of bark. "In retrospect," he wrote, "I think I was unwise in not insisting on my own plan: that we should all go over the Mamba and live out the war in the Ioma district." He gave in when the soldiers said that they were under orders to return to Port Moresby by the fastest possible route.

Before dawn he woke the Sisters and said the Mass of St Laurence. Then as dawn was breaking they all slipped quietly down the river by canoe. They met up with the soldiers later that day, and the following morning they all set out. Within four days they reached the Japanese lines near Popondetta. Then one of the guides suddenly announced his intention of going to see where the Japanese were, and before anyone could stop him he had gone. One of the local men warned that the guide had probably gone to tell the Japanese where they all were.

They decided to abandon their former plan, to retrace their

steps, and cross the road from Gona nearer to the sea than they had intended. This meant bypassing the inland mission stations of Sangara and Isivita. By morning they felt safe from pursuit from Popondetta and rested until noon. Early in the afternoon they set out for the Gona road and before long were within a few hundred yards of their objective. Before they could move farther the rearguard came running up and gasped out that the Japanese were approaching from behind. All quickly fell into the positions they had rehearsed should they be attacked. A tense wait followed, but there was no sign of the Japanese. One of the scouts then reported that all was clear. The forward scout took another look at the road, and when he too reported all clear the group of people ran hastily across and into the bush on the other side and kept running for ten minutes before stopping to catch their breath.

Father Benson recalled shaking Lieutenant Smith by the hand and saying, "That's our biggest hurdle crossed." The girls were smiling and chatting gaily.

Then came the shatter of rifle fire. We spun round and before I dived headlong into the bush my mind registered the scene in exact detail; the eighteen or twenty Japanese, with rifles to their shoulders, ranged along the edge of a clearing less than fifty yards away. I remember Miss Hayman crying out; I remember her starting to run, then she seemed to spin round and fall. I dived into the bush. I was still clutching my blue canvas bag, but I had lost my hat, and I remember that this, for some peculiar reason, disturbed me. I crouched down low, and began to work my way sideways towards the place where I thought Miss Hayman had fallen. I heard more rifle fire away to my right; but of the others I saw nothing. It was growing dark now. I called softly, but there was no reply.

Father Benson was in the jungle for six days and five nights without food before he was captured by the Japanese. Sister Hayman was with the rest of the party when they retreated through the bush and managed to evade the Japanese. That night they rested in the jungle and in the early morning moved on and soon found a village. Two of the men from the Papuan Infantry Battalion were still with them, and they offered to go into the village. On learning that the people seemed friendly, the rest of the party went in as well. It was the village of Upper Dobodura, and the people were playing football. The Papuan Infantry Battalion men began to suspect that all was not well, and they warned Lieutenant Smith who asked for carriers to help with two of the wounded men. These the villagers promised to supply the following morning. That night the party slept outside the village.

In the morning, very early, they called for the carriers, but none was forthcoming. There were delays and excuses, and at about nine o'clock Lieutenant Smith decided they must push on without help. They took it in turns to carry the wounded men, four men to each, with the girls doing what they could to help. Progress was slow. What the party did not know was that a boy of the village had been sent to Popondetta to tell the Japanese that the party was in the vicinity. As the party was leaving, another man ran down the road to meet the Japanese and tell them to hurry up. The party had not gone more than a few miles along the road towards the Managalas country, away from Popondetta, when the Japanese patrol caught up and opened fire with machine-guns.

Lieutenant Smith and the two girls who were in the front managed to find cover in the bush. According to a report made just after the end of the war, the rest of the soldiers knelt or fell on the ground and returned the Japanese fire, fighting until all were killed or wounded. The Japanese rushed in and bayoneted those who were still alive. Lieutenant Smith was separated from the Sisters, who wandered in the bush all night, finding themselves in the morning back at the village from which they had come. A friendly man saw them and went out to them with a warning not to come into the village. He brought them some pawpaw and, while they were eating it, he went away and found two small boys whom he sent to guide them to a village some distance away. Here they were to be given into the hands of a village councillor who would conduct them to the Managalas from whence they could make their way to safety.

The councillor was found in his garden, and that night the Sisters slept in the garden house with the women and children. Everything was very friendly. In the morning the councillor bade them get ready and they started out, as they supposed, to the Managalas. The man, however, was a person with a grudge against a white man, and he was venting his resentment against the two women as a "pay-back". He took them by other tracks back to Popondetta. Two small boys, realizing what was happening, ran back to the friendly native, their relative at Upper Dobodura, and reported. He hurried along to see if he could intercept them, but he reached Popondetta only to find the Sisters were already prisoners. It was evening and he crept to the coffee house where they were and made signs to them to come, but they waved him away. He feared to speak to them or make a noise, but he stayed in the bush close by all night. The Japanese guards did not ill-treat the Sisters, other than to proffer food and water to them, and then snatch it away as they put out a hand to take it.

Early in the morning the friendly native again went to the coffee house in an attempt to get the Sisters away, but they made urgent signs to him to go away. They were sitting on the floor — "and it was very fearful, they were weeping".

At about 8 a.m. four Japanese soldiers passed his hiding-place. Two of them carried rifles and two had shovels. They signalled to the Sisters to come out, and they took them away into the Ururu Plantation, which was close to the coffee house. Here was a freshly dug grave. One of the soldiers approached Mavis Parkinson and attempted to embrace her. She resisted, and he stepped backward and plunged his bayonet into her side. She fell to the ground. Sister Hayman moaned and lifted a towel or cloth to her face, and her escort plunged his bayonet with an upward plunge into her throat.

"They both died immediately, and the Japanese, two to each body, lifted them and dropped them into the grave, one on top of the other, and covered them with a little earth."

Lieutenant Smith wandered in the jungle for some days and was found by two boys who took him to a garden near Sangara and fed him. Two natives came and spoke to him in police Motu. They both had rifles. Smith had his gun beside him. The two natives "jumped" him, having grabbed his gun. He was taken to Embogi, the councillor and sorcerer (sometimes described as an "ex-policeman with a grudge") who had been responsible for the betrayal of the white missionaries. The Japanese had bribed Embogi with an Emperor's Ring and promises of a high position. Embogi took Lieutenant Smith to the Japanese at Buna. A Japanese diary of this time records, "A prisoner who was brought in by natives yesterday was beheaded this morning."

Papuan Christians took careful note of the spot where the

Sisters were buried. Fighting in the area ceased on 22nd January 1943, and the bodies were exhumed for identification in February. They were taken to Sangara mission station, where they were reinterred. Over the grave were placed two crosses marked simply:

MAY HAYMAN   MAVIS PARKINSON
August 1942   August 1942

OF SANGARA AND ISIVITA

Mission work in the Sangara district was begun in 1922 by a layman, Henry Holland, ably assisted by a Papuan teacher, Andrew Uware. Besides being a new district, the work was new in another sense. It was the first attempt to erect a head-station any great distance from the coast. The great obstacle to opening up the area was transport. Sangara was twenty-seven miles from the coast and everything had to be brought in by carriers.

Within two years Henry Holland had a road under construction. It ran from Gona through the swamps and then up the long, gradual incline to Sangara, crossing a multitude of little creeks which, after a heavy fall of rain, became rushing torrents. More than forty years later the road is still in use. When it was repaired after the war, the foundations were found still to be good, and the ditches needed little more than cleaning out. It was the work of a man who had only primitive natives as helpers, and in an area where there is practically no stone.

Henry Holland had joined the New Guinea Mission in 1910, coming from sheep country in inland New South Wales. He had worked first at Ambasi with Copland King, and it was there that he made the acquaintance of Andrew Uware, who was to be his lifelong friend, helper and companion. Henry Holland was a quiet, slow-spoken man, quite unimpressive to meet, but a giant in his capacity for work and for thoroughness in everything he undertook. He never appeared to be in a hurry, and often seemed exasperatingly slow to his fellow workers, who consequently were apt to misjudge him at first and to underestimate his worth. He took a pride in doing a good job and never let speed become a substitute for efficiency. Bridges built by him were said to be models of strength and stability and were known far and wide in pre-vehicular days when bridges were almost non-existent, and one waded through rivers, or sat and waited until floods subsided.

In his spiritual work he was even more meticulous. Painstakingly he learnt the language of the people, so that he could gain entry to their thought and hearts. For long hours into the night he worked, translating the Scriptures and church services into the language of the people. In the church and in the school he taught and retaught with Andrew Uware by his side. Since Andrew was an Ambasi man, he also had to learn the language of the Sangara people.

Once the work at Sangara had been firmly established, Henry Holland moved farther inland and began in 1928 a new station at Isivita dedicated to St Michael and All Angels. Isivita was a two-hour walk from Sangara along a track that twisted its way through dense rain forest on the lower slopes of Mount Lamington. The walker had to cross many deep gullies — down one side, through the water at the bottom, and then up a steep bank. In 1938 Bishop Strong, realizing the tremendous contribution Henry Holland could make as a priest to mission work in the Sangara and Isivita areas, ordained him to the sacred ministry, after giving him a special course of instruction.

In a letter to a friend in the year of his ordination, Father Holland wrote, "You will have met our Bishop and he may have told you of the recent baptisms at Sangara and Isivita. Father James Benson came up (from Gona) to Sangara when the time came and assisted me with the baptism of ninety-three adults. Two weeks afterwards I baptized twenty-three infants and small children. Yesterday, St Michael and All Angels' Day, was our Patronal festival day. We had Holy Communion at 7 a.m. with catechumens present until after the address and an open air service at 10 a.m. Altogether there were about seven hundred persons present. We have much to be thankful for. The people are willing, and many keen to hear and to be baptized."

When Henry Holland moved farther inland to open up the station at Isivita in 1928, Nurse Margery Brenchley and Miss Lilla Lashmar took over charge of Sangara mission station. Henry Holland, stationed a few miles away round the base of the mountain, became their helper and adviser, and he still retained contact with the Sangara people, to whom he gave religious instruction, especially in the school.

Sangara was a lovely station. It was in the centre of a large coffee- and rubber-growing area worked co-operatively by the government and local people. Ten miles away in a direct line, but two days' travel up and down the endless gullies, was Mount Lamington, dark on the shadowed ridge, sometimes blue and sharp, often swathed with thin scarves of mist.

Born in England, Margery Brenchley was the eldest of four children. While still in her teens she had come to Australia with her brother. She felt that nursing was her vocation and entered the Brisbane Hospital for training. During her four years there she attended Holy Trinity Church at Fortitude Valley where she was influenced both by Canon J. Needham, later Chairman of the Australian Board of Missions, and the Rector, the Reverend S. Watkin. When she left for New Guinea in 1927 the parish adopted her as their "own missionary" and contributed to her support from then until the time of her death.

Those who knew her as mission nurse described her as slightly built, wiry, usually dressed in brown, with dark hair and eyes, and tirelessly devoted to the care of the native people. When she arrived in New Guinea, the native "doctors", who combined sorcery with their New Guinea medicine, held sway over the greater part of the country. She was at first stationed at Dogura and while there built up a confidence based on personal friendship with the women of Wedau.

Lilla Lashmar was a South Australian from the parish of St Cuthbert's, Prospect. She had spent most of her childhood on Kangaroo Island and had later worked in an office in Adelaide as a comptometrist. It was after attending a mission conducted by Canon Needham that she felt the call to missionary service, and on his advice she did a course of teacher-training at St Cuthbert's Day School before going to the A.B.M. training college for her mission training. While at the college she earned money to pay her fees by making and selling baskets.

Miss Lashmar was posted to Gona station in December 1929, and then spent some time at Dogura before being sent to work at Sangara with Sister Brenchley. The two women, with Henry Holland at Isivita some miles away, were the only European members of the mission in the inland. The nearest mission station was Gona and the nearest government station was Buna, a few miles to the south of Gona.

All supplies coming up on the mission vessel from Samarai were landed at Gona, or at Sanananda a few miles nearer to Buna, where the mission had a store shed on the beach. Sanananda was then a port of call for coastal boats, for from it the rough road ran inland to the coffee plantations near Sangara, and down this road the bags of coffee were brought on a lorry for loading on the boats. But whether landed at Gona or Sanananda, the boxes had to be opened and the contents repacked into smaller bundles more suited for carrying, for usually this task fell on the shoulders of a small army of mission-boys, who had come down to act as "carriers". This was no mean task, for the return journey was all uphill, at first through swampy bog, then up and down endless ridges and gullies, in places wading up icy, swift-flowing streams, over rugged rocks and slippery twisted roots, up into the foothills upon which Sangara station was built.

In these circumstances only the smaller things and absolute necessities could be carried. Equipment for the school or dispensary — blackboards, sterilizer machine, a stove — would be left for the men who would take them to pieces, as far as possible, and bind them to poles for carrying by two or more men apiece. Furniture for the mission house, such as cupboards, beds, stools, tables and chairs, were made from bush timber on the spot, or constructed of packing-cases in which goods had been sent.

One of the present writers recalls relieving Margery Brenchley, who had gone south for medical treatment. Her instructions were to take everything from her previous station. She still recalls the horrified look on Lilla Lashmar's face as she sighted the luggage coming off the boat. "Who ever told you to bring all that stuff?" she asked indignantly. "Don't you realize that mission-boys carry all our baggage on their *backs*?" The next two days were spent in undoing everything and repacking the bare necessities into the smallest and lightest containers. The rest of the luggage was left at Gona.

Lilla Lashmar had a heart-breaking job in many respects. The school buildings had not been built to hold the three to four hundred children whose names were on the roll, nor were there teachers enough for half that number. Most communication with the missionaries on the coast was by letter, sent by special messenger or by the regular police "mail-man", who walked from Buna to Kokoda to meet his counterpart from Port Moresby. At Kokoda an exchange of mailbags was made, the Buna policeman bringing back the mail from Port Moresby and the outside world, and the Port Moresby policeman taking out the mail for posting.

If Lilla Lashmar or Margery Brenchley wished to visit missionaries at Gona or farther down the coast they had to face the ordeal of walking down the twenty-seven-mile track through the gullies and streams, making a pause at Popondetta — at that time only a clearing with a half-caste's house, a small rest-house, and a few drying racks on which coffee beans were spread for drying before being bagged. This was known as the "depot", where the coffee was collected and taken down to the coast for shipping. The lorry-driver and his wife were the only people living there. The missionaries, if lucky, might get a ride for at least part of the way, always with the possibility of the lorry being bogged on the low-lying coastal flats. Sometimes Nurse Brenchley faced the journey with a sick patient she was trying to get to Gona for a doctor's attention.

The village coffee gardens contributed greatly towards the self-respect of the people of the Sangara area. The men of the villages worked on a roster, each village providing men for a week's work in turn, thus keeping up a continuous stream of labour. When the crop was harvested and sold, all had a share in the proceeds. The supervisor of the coffee gardens was Captain Louis Austen, a former master of a coastal vessel, who managed Higaturu, a coffee and rubber plantation a mile or so to the back of Sangara. Sometimes Nurse Brenchley and Lilla Lashmar walked over the hills to pay a visit to Captain Austen's wife.

From 1938 to 1941 Father Henry Holland was priest for Sangara and Isivita. In August 1941 Father Vivian Redlich, an Englishman educated at Oakham and St John's, Leatherhead, was appointed priest-in-charge of the Sangara district. His first curacy had been at Dewsbury Moor, Yorkshire; then he joined a Queensland bush brotherhood and for five years served in the Dawson and Callide valleys, with an area as large as six northern counties of England under his charge. The scattered people amounted to about six thousand. His transport was an old Model T Ford, and he would spend a week-end at each of his centres, holding services and Sunday school each Sunday.

At the beginning of each month he would load up his Model T outside the brotherhood house — now St Barnabas's Vicarage, North Rockhampton — with his portable altar (designed by himself), vestments and church linen, a crowbar, pick, shovel, and axe, as well as a complete kit of car tools. With two canvas water-bags attached to the front fender and a supply of iron rations, he would be ready to start on his rounds. Most of the country through which he passed was very rough and the roads but roads in name.

The Model T was the joy of Brother Vivian's heart, and every trip an adventure. Another Brother, the Reverend C. N. Lavender, recalls a trip he made with Vivian Redlich: "The road was terrible, and there was thirty miles of it! I recall Vivian, chin up, head back, pipe tightly clenched between his teeth, throwing the hand-throttle to the full, and going for all he was worth, and for all he could get out of the car. For the whole thirty miles I could not get in a word of conversation on account of the noisy bumping, but Vivian talked all the way. At the end of the run I remarked that I had only touched the seat about twice on the way, and he retorted, 'Well at least that will save the upholstery!' The uphols-tery consisted of a folded sack."

The brotherhood were "sometimes glad of the quiet which followed his hilarious end-of-month stays at the brotherhood house". The quiet was particularly appreciated by a Brother who was a noted heavy sleeper. Brother Vivian invented a gadget which he attached to an alarm clock. When the alarm went off it released a knocker, opened a door and lifted open a window beside the sleeper's head.

Vivian Redlich was a very thin man, not very strong, and inclined to discipline himself into doing things that seemed to be beyond his strength. His eyesight was weak and he wore very thick glasses. He had an impulsive manner of speaking which sometimes brought words tumbling out in an embarrassing splutter. The brotherhood, seeing a man with so many physical disadvantages attempt and do so much, were spurred on to many things they might not otherwise have accomplished.

Vivian Redlich served five years with the brotherhood on a stipend of £50 a year and bound by the vows of poverty, chastity and obedience. He was due for leave in England but instead offered for work with the New Guinea Mission. Without any holiday break he left the brotherhood house and sailed for Papua. He began his missionary life at Dogura and then went on to Gona. While there he was sent on loan to Taupota to supervise the repair and strengthening of the church roof and walls, which were in a dangerous condition.

In August 1941 he was appointed priest-in-charge of the Sangara district, relieving Father Henry Holland of that responsibility. Within a short time he was writing to his father that he had a "swanky hospital" nearly completed, a teacher's house, new wash-house, stores for coconuts, firewood and garden tools, and a priest's house and workshop in preparation. He was proud of his electric plant with its new parts constructed "mostly out of scraps of oddments and tin cans".

When, a few months later, the war came to New Guinea, the staff at Sangara decided to follow the mission policy of staying on their station. The mission continued to function normally, priest, nurse and teacher going about their various duties. In June 1942 Bishop Strong, while paying a visit to Sangara, decided that Father Redlich's health was unsatisfactory and that he should go back with the Bishop to Dogura for a rest and a change. During Vivian Redlich's brief call at Gona he managed to persuade May Hayman to consent to an engagement, and her acceptance filled him with a desire to tell the whole world of his amazing good fortune. At Wanigela he came along the beach with eyes shining and face beaming, almost shouting the good news, "May and I are engaged!" He and Sister May Hayman were never to see each other again.

Just before the outbreak of war Father Holland was joined at Isivita by John Duffill, a Queenslander from the parish of Holy Trinity, Wooloongabba, South Brisbane. His mother had died when he was seven years old, but when his father married again two years later, a loving stepmother cared for the six children of his former marriage, the eldest of whom was thirteen years old.

John sang in the Holy Trinity choir as a boy soprano, and later became a server, and, in time, head server. He was a keen Boy Scout in the Holy Trinity troop and afterward became Scout-master of the first Kangaroo Point troop. The Rector of Holy Trinity, the Reverend Canon C. Edwards, took a keen interest in the boys of the parish and his influence had a great deal to do with John Duffill's decision to become a missionary. John discussed the whole matter with his younger sister, who had been considering taking the same step. Their father had recently died and the two young people decided that it would be wrong to leave their step-mother alone. It would then be better for John to be the one to go. He arrived in Papua in 1938 and soon found himself called upon for a wide variety of tasks. A layman with the New Guinea Mission might find himself required to look after cattle, build houses, attend to vehicles or machinery (especially when broken down), supervise gardens, look after pressure lamps and "fridges", take over the management of a boat, give medical aid, teach in a school, look after a plantation, build a bridge or make a road.

John Duffill was responsible for the building of the Sefoa mission house, and was then given the supervision of the mission vessel, the *Maclaren King*. The mission boats had been under the care of a European or half-European skipper since early times, who had charge of the boat on its six-weekly trips up and down the coast, carrying mail, stores and passengers to all the stations, bringing back cargoes of copra, etc., to Samarai. The Bishop asked John to act as manager and general supervisor: to attend to the loading and unloading, checking of cargo as it was unloaded on the beaches or wharves along the coast, caring for the well-being of the passengers, white and brown. Although he was no seaman and had no active part in the navigation, John had an over-all responsibility towards the ship and crew, passengers and stores, timing of arrival and departure.

It was in March 1942 when John was on his last trip up the coast with Bishop Strong as passenger that a Japanese aircraft attacked the *Maclaren King* off Buna, dropping bombs and swooping low to machine-gun the crew and passengers in the dinghy. The boys dived overboard and submerged, while the Bishop and John landed and made for shelter among trees on the beach, throwing themselves flat on the sand when bullets pelted around them, then rising and running between the bursts of fire.

By now Rabaul had been captured and all of New Britain was in enemy hands. Bombs were being dropped on Port Moresby as the raids became more and more frequent. The Bishop continued on his way to Wanigela where the staff, hearing of the attack on the *Maclaren King*, was in a state of some anxiety. He made light of the incident, but praised the presence of mind of the crew-boys and the calmness of John Duffill during the attack.

John went on to Isivita where he had been appointed to assist Father Henry Holland, to teach in the school and to carry out some building. The presence of another European on the mission station was a great boon to the ageing missionary, who had spent so many years without white companionship, but it was to be a short-lived association.

When on 21st July the Japanese made the sudden landing at Gona, which was the prelude towards their rapid advance to Kokoda, Mr Harry Bitmead, a government medical assistant, notified Nurse Brenchley and Miss Lashmar. Earlier the two women had declined the offer of an Australian officer to escort them over the Owen Stanleys to Port Moresby. Now their post lay in the way of an advancing army. They sent a runner through the bush track to Isivita to ask Father Holland what they should do and, on receiving no reply, packed a few belongings and prepared to set out for Isivita.

At Isivita, Father Holland had no hesitation in making his decision to stay. John Duffill had already refused to leave for his furlough, believing that his place was to remain in the diocese; but the priest was worried about two things. He feared that the local people would be punished if they did not hand over the white missionaries to the Japanese. And he believed that Nurse Brenchley and Miss Lashmar, for whom he felt a responsibility in the absence of Father Redlich, should be taken to safety.

On the night that Father Benson, Sister Hayman and Mavis Parkinson were trying to avoid capture along the Gona road, Father Holland saw to it that the entire staff of Isivita mission station went off to sleep in their garden houses in the bush. He stayed on the station and slept as usual in the mission house.

Early the next morning, 22nd July, the staff began to build a secret camp for themselves in the bush and also, at another place, a shelter for the two women expected from Sangara and for John Duffill. Later in the morning Nurse Brenchley and Lilla Lashmar arrived, accompanied by Lucian Tapiedi, a young Papuan just beginning his career as a teacher. Lucian Tapiedi was the nephew of a suspected sorcerer of Taupota in the Milne Bay district. At the mission school he had been influenced by Miss Nita Inman, the

*The sanctuary of the Cathedral of St Peter and St Paul, Dogura.
The mural is the work of Canon James Benson.*

*Bishop David Hand, then assistant bishop of the diocese,
with chiefs, village policemen, and evangelists.*

The consecration of the first Papuan Bishop, the Right Reverend George Ambo, in St John
Anglican Cathedral, Brisbane. He is led by the then Bishop of New Guinea, the Rig
Reverend Philip Strong (left), and the Assistant Bishop, the Right Reverend David Har
(right). They are preceded by the Reverend Bevan Meredith.

schoolteacher, and by the Reverend Edwin Nuagoro, the Papuan priest. He attended St Aidan's Teacher Training College at Divari, and graduated as a teacher-evangelist in 1941. Appointed to Sangara to work with Lilla Lashmar in the large school, he soon fitted happily into the life of the mission.

For the rest of the week that marked the Japanese landing at Gona, the two women, John Duffill and Lucian Tapiedi remained in the bush in one place, the remainder of the Isivita staff camped elsewhere, while Father Holland stayed on the station. Daily, Lucian and Andrew Uware made trips to the mission to bring food supplies to those in hiding.

It became evident that this dangerous state of affairs could not continue. The numbers of Japanese moving up the road were daily increasing, and parties of them were sallying along tracks leading into the bush, with intent to rout out any Europeans who might be in hiding. There was little hope of remaining undetected, and moreover any loyal natives who wished to help the Europeans by hiding or feeding them were in danger of cruel reprisals from the Japanese if caught. Father Holland, who passionately desired to remain with his people, realized at this stage that the best way of helping them was by moving right out of their area. Left to themselves, they would be comparatively safe, for the Japanese would probably not molest them, beyond taking their food or compelling them to work for them. He talked the situation over with Andrew Uware, who agreed with him, and advised him to get away from Isivita and to take the other missionaries with him.

On the day of the landing at Gona, Father Redlich was returning by boat from Dogura greatly improved in health. The boat on which he travelled discovered Japanese ships at Buna, so hastily retreated to a small cove, where stores for an army unit were taken ashore and hidden under cover of darkness. The boat was to return to Dogura, and Father Redlich could have returned on it. He did not know how far the Japanese had penetrated. He could not be sure whether the Sangara staff were still there. He made his decision to find his way back to the station and managed to get safely through the Japanese lines and into his own district.

Mr Bitmead, the government medical assistant, who had warned the two women at Sangara, had himself been captured by the Japanese, but escaped and was cared for by some of the local

E

people. On the Saturday following the landing at Gona he was told that Father Redlich had eluded the Japanese and was living in a banana-leaf shelter not a great distance from Sangara. Mr Bitmead set off to the hide-out and on the way bypassed Sangara mission station, now deserted because the Japanese had told the local people of their intention to destroy the station the very next day, Sunday.

Late that night the medical assistant stumbled into Father Redlich's hide-out. After seeing that Harry Bitmead had been given food, Father Redlich turned to the crowd of people standing at the entrance and told them that he would celebrate the Holy Communion the following morning as it would be Sunday. This involved his return to the mission station to get vestments and other things that he needed. It was about midnight when he left. While he was away Mr Bitmead rested.

When Father Redlich returned he woke his visitor, and the two men sat talking about the priest's journey to Sangara, the presence of the Japanese already on the mission station, the Japanese advance in Papua, and the future. Just before dawn a local man ran into the shelter and cried, "Father! Mr Bitmead! Go! Do not wait here! One man, Embogi, has been watching the shelter all night and has gone to report you to the Japanese!"

Father Redlich bowed his head in prayer for a moment and then asked, "Why has Embogi done this? We have never harmed him."

In reply the people told him that Embogi resented the presence and influence of the Christian missionaries and that he wanted to make himself king of that part of Papua.

Then Father Redlich turned to the crowd and said that the day was Sunday, the Lord's Day, and that he would have Mass as planned. He then vested and began the service. Many people in the crowd came forward to receive communion. At the conclusion of the service Father Redlich and Mr Bitmead packed a few things in two rice bags and set off towards a village about five hours' walk away where, they had been told, Captain Austen was hiding. Mrs Austen had been evacuated and the captain was in hiding with his assistant, Mr Anthony Gors, a mixed-race man, and Gors's wife and son.

Late in the afternoon of that Sunday they reached the hide-out and found Captain Austen and the others there. They were given mugs of tea, and while they sat drinking and talking they were interrupted by a boy rushing in and shouting, "The Japs are coming! The Japs are coming!"

Captain Austen handed Mr Bitmead a gun, and together they went out a little distance along the track, leaving Father Redlich in the shelter. He had said that he would not take up arms against anyone. The other two waited, one on either side of the track. Soon they heard a voice, "Don't shoot, Aussie! Don't shoot, Aussie!"

Captain Austen motioned to his companion to keep quiet and to remain concealed. Soon an American airman staggered along the track past them. The two men allowed him to pass and then, having cast a quick look back down the track, followed him to the shelter. There they learnt that he had been on a bombing mission and that his plane had been shot down. He thought that he was the only survivor, but about an hour later another member of the crew stumbled into the hide-out. It was decided that the group of people should split up. Mr Bitmead opted in favour of attempting to cross the Owen Stanleys with the two Americans, who were under orders to return to Port Moresby by the fastest possible route. Captain Austen and the others with him thought they would try to walk to Oro Bay and from there travel by boat along the coast. This was a much easier prospect *if* they could manage to get all the way to Oro Bay and *if* they managed to find a boat that would take them.

Father Redlich's aim was to join up with the rest of the missionaries from Sangara and Isivita. Before Harry Bitmead left, Vivian Redlich gave him a letter he had written to his father in England.* As the medical assistant looked back towards the shelter he saw Father Redlich standing, watching him, and called out, "Good luck and God bless you!"

This was the last meeting of the two men. Writing much later, Mr Bitmead, who succeeded in getting to Port Moresby, said of Father Redlich: "He was a great man and a saintly man. In all my dealings with him I found he had a great charity and a real love for his fellow men."

As Father Redlich celebrated the Holy Communion in the hide-

Appendix B. The Reverend Vivian Redlich's letter, held in St. Paul's Cathedral, London.

out near Sangara on Sunday, 26th July 1942, so did Father Holland in the Church of St Michael at Isivita. Unknown to the worshippers inside the church, some members of the Papuan Infantry Battalion arrived and stood guard while the service was in progress, lest there should be a surprise attack by the Japanese, who were now spread out along the Kokoda road less than six miles away.

Later in the morning there was a fight between some Japanese and Allied aircraft almost overhead at Isivita. At least one Australian plane was shot down. The people at Isivita saw the plane on fire and losing height, and then saw a white parachute billowing as the pilot baled out. Later in the afternoon the pilot was brought to Father Holland by some of the local people. His name was Johnson. He had baled out of his plane and had landed in a tree some miles from Isivita. Hearing someone approaching and fearing it might be the Japanese, he took out his gun, but it was a local Orokaiva man who, in faltering English, said that he would take the Australian to the mission at Isivita. There were many small bush tracks leading to the station, so they had no difficulty in avoiding the Japanese. They were met by Father Holland, but the pilot was so anxious to be on his way to Port Moresby that he stayed only long enough for food. His plan was to use map and compass and walk across the Owen Stanleys. He had not been gone long when a second airman walked into the station. He also was a victim of the morning encounter with the Japanese. Despite the fact that it was already twilight and night was rapidly closing in, he decided to set off after Johnson in the hope that they would together make their way to Port Moresby.

On the Monday morning some people from Mumuni village brought in a badly wounded American airman. He was one of two who had been involved in a plane crash the previous day. The other had been killed in the crash and buried near the village. Father Holland realized that there was little that could be done for the airman. He watched over him throughout the night and went to rest in the morning while Andrew Uware watched over the now delirious man. At about 10 a.m. the airman died.

Father Holland was now increasingly concerned that the presence of Europeans might cause reprisals by the Japanese among the local people. The arrival of the Australian airmen and the death of the American had made it clear that the war was

sweeping down on Isivita. He sent for Andrew and told him of
the arrival of Father Redlich at the secret camp and his fears for
the safety of the people. Andrew Uware advised Father Holland
to leave Isivita and to take the two women to safety with the
other missionaries, suggesting that they should go along a track
that would take them round the base of Mount Lamington not
far from Sangara but far enough for it to be unlikely that the
Japanese would be there. They could then make their way into
the district known as the Managalas. From there they could cross
the Owen Stanleys at a point where it would not be so difficult
for the two women.

On Friday or Saturday of that week, ten days after the landing
at Gona, the party of missionaries, Father Holland, Father Redlich, John Duffill, Lucian Tapiedi, Margery Brenchley and Lilla
Lashmar, set off from Isivita. Before leaving, Father Holland
gave Andrew Uware complete charge over the mission storeroom,
telling him to do with it as he thought best but that he should not
let it fall into the hands of the Japanese. Their route carried them
back towards Sangara but in much closer to the top of the volcano
than the track they usually followed. Throughout the day they
walked, going round the base of Mount Lamington, a walk that
must have been very tiring to Lilla and Margery because of the
vast number of creeks and gullies that had to be crossed, and the
unpleasant conditions underfoot.

In the afternoon they arrived at a village called Sehaparete,
where they were greeted by a young married woman, a very close
friend of Andrew Uware's family. She saw to it that the party was
fed and sheltered for the night. The next morning Father Holland
asked the men of the village if some of them would help carry
packages, but received no response. Instead, the men told him that
the day of Europeans in Papua was over, that the spirits of their
dead relations and friends were returning dressed as soldiers and
that soon ships and planes would come bearing great quantities
of valuable cargo. Father Holland was surprised and shocked, and
told the people that they were foolish to believe such rubbish. One
of the men became so angry that he struck Father Holland on the
face, knocking him to the ground. The friendly young woman
intervened and asked her husband to carry for the missionaries.
With this man helping them, the missionaries set off in the direction of another village called Sewa. From this village they were

supposed to turn off into the Managalas and eventually make their way over the mountains.

However, somewhere between Sehaparete and Sewa the party of missionaries met up with Captain Austen's party, whose unfortunate plan was to try to reach Oro Bay and from there escape to Tufi or some other place of safety. Captain Austen prevailed upon the missionaries to join him in his attempt to reach the coast, and so they all arrived together as one party at Perombata, having spent one night at Vurante on the way.

At Perombata the attitude of the villagers was, to outward appearances, what it always was when they received visitors. The party spent some time in the village, sleeping there for three nights. One man offered to take them by a bush track to some garden land at the headwaters of Eroro Creek, and from there they would then be able to make their way with caution to the bay. Eroro mission station near Oro Bay was only a few days' walk away, but the missionaries were probably unaware that the mission had already been entered by a party of Japanese and that the missionary and his wife had escaped only by a small margin of time, through the loyalty of a church councillor who had warned them and taken them to a cave for safety until the raiders had departed. Then they returned to their station to gather food and a few necessities for an overland journey to Wanigela, a station in Collingwood Bay still untouched by the Japanese. Thus there would have been no Europeans at Eroro to welcome the party from Isivita and no certainty of a boat to take them on from Oro Bay.

Unknown to the party, the news of their arrival and stay at Perombata had filtered down the track ahead of them and had come to the ears of a man called Pauembo of Embi village. Pauembo was one of a group in that area who had been approached by the Japanese and told that they should bring to the Japanese any Europeans who were in the vicinity. Equally unknown to the party was the fact that several meetings were held at Perombata at which Pauembo made it quite clear to the people that the Japanese would surely punish all of them if they did not hand the Europeans over. Although many showed reluctance and would have preferred to see the Europeans safely to Oro Bay, it was decided that, in order to protect the whole village, the Europeans be handed over. It was also decided that the actual capture would not take place in Perombata itself, and it seems that the villagers hoped that they would be able to keep the realization of just what was happening from the party for some time. In the village constable's book Captain Austen wrote, "People friendly but not helpful."

The morning after the third night spent in the village the party set out for what they hoped was one of the last stages on their way to freedom. Some time after leaving Perombata they crossed Jewaia Creek. Here one of the carriers offered to take Captain Austen's rifle, a normal thing to do for the stones at this crossing were particularly slippery. It may or may not have occurred to the party that they were handing over their only means of defence and that henceforth they were at the mercy of their guides.

They had travelled some distance beyond the creek when it was discovered that a box containing station records and money had been left behind. Lucian volunteered to go back for it. Nearing Jewaia Creek, Lucian was met by a small group of men. What happened remains partly a matter for conjecture, though later evidence suggests that the Perombata escort believed that Lucian Tapiedi would realize something was wrong before they neared the Japanese and that the box had been left by design rather than accident. It is possible that the second group of men had intended to give Lucian, the Papuan, a choice, plainly telling him of their intentions regarding the Europeans and giving him the alternatives of either siding with the Europeans or against them.

Lucian Tapiedi was killed with an axe there on the track and his body was buried nearby. In 1943 it was removed to a grave in the churchyard at Sangara, where it rests beside those of Sister May Hayman and Mavis Parkinson. All three were later covered by the dust and ash thrown out of the volcano on Mount Lamington. The spot where Lucian was killed on the track near Jewaia Creek is marked by a cross.

The party of whites and their escort went on to Kurumbo and from there to Hanakiro, where all rested and drank from coconuts. At Warisota Plantation one of the women became ill and was placed upon a hastily constructed litter and carried as far as Embi, where a stop was made for the night. Here the whites were given food and a guard placed around the rest-house. The people from Perombata were joined by men from Boro, probably led by Piremi, a man to whom the Japanese had spoken. Several of the women at Embi tried to help Lilla and Margery but to little avail, though one old woman stayed with them all night.

At Embi the "handing-over" took place, the Perombata men returning to their village and the Boro men taking charge of the "captives". The next morning the party set off, not in the direction of Eroro, but towards Dobodura. Soon after leaving Boro, the party's bags and bundles disappeared. The failure of Lucian to return would have been at least the first warning of unfriendly intentions, the loss of their bags and bundles of belongings the second.

At the Samboga River the women were carried across while men waded through. At Dobodura tea was made for all to drink before going on to Sinemi. Here another halt was made for a short time, and then the party moved on to the cross-roads at Jeropa where the Europeans were handed over to Japanese soldiers. After more soldiers arrived at Jeropa, the captives were put in a truck and driven off to Buna.

At the camp at Buna the party was questioned. Why did they run away if they really were missionaries? Margery Brenchley answered, "We did not run away from you, but as we heard the shooting getting nearer we went away to be safe from that." After the interrogation there is little detailed information. Japanese war diaries record that they were all beheaded on the beach near Buna by a Japanese soldier who volunteered for the terrifying operation.

The sands of Buna beach are grey. The blue sea laps the shore and there is always the rich beauty of the wild beach flowers. There were ended the lives of Margery Brenchley, nurse, Lilla Lashmar, teacher, Henry Holland and Vivian Redlich, priests, John Duffill, missionary, Captain Louis Austen, Mr Tony Gors, his wife and little son.

"I turned away for the sight sickened me," records one Japanese diary. Another states that the last to be executed was the young son of Tony Gors.

The execution took place between 12th and 14th August 1942. The bodies of the entire party disappeared, and it is presumed that they were thrown into the sea.

Blessed are the dead which die in the Lord; even so saith the Spirit; for they rest from their labours.

OF PORT MORESBY AND BOIANAI

Henry Matthews gave thirty-three years of his life to missionary service, first on the Aboriginal mission at Mitchell River on the west coast of Cape York, then in New Guinea. He was born in Victoria in 1876 and went to Mitchell River as superintendent in 1904. In 1915 he married a fellow missionary and in 1919, after undergoing a theological course in Melbourne, was ordained to the ministry. In 1927 he became Rector of Port Moresby, and spent much of his time travelling up and down the coast, performing baptisms and marriages and caring for his flock. Only twice during his ministry did he go on leave, and that at intervals of ten years.

In 1939 he was commissioned as a chaplain by the Army, but when, after the Japanese entry into the war, he was told that he was a year over the military retiring age and would have to retire he appealed, unsuccessfully, to the Primate and the Bishop of New Guinea. By this time most of the civilian population of Port Moresby had been evacuated, and Japanese planes were making daily and nightly raids. His wife had died, his daughters had gone to Australia, and his son, in government service, had been stationed at Daru, in the Gulf district of Papua.

When the final decision was made that he should retire on 8th August 1942 Father Matthews was very distressed. He sought for and was given permission to accompany a boatload of some ninety mixed-race people to Daru, hoping that he might see his son there, and that he could help and comfort the displaced people who were being evacuated by military orders.

On the journey he was accompanied by Leslie Gariadi, a young Papuan teacher-evangelist from Boianai, who after his training at St Aidan's College, Dogura, had been sent to Port Moresby to assist Father Matthews.

Near Bramble Bay the *Mumutu*, the ship in which the party was travelling, was bombed by a Japanese aircraft and sunk. The only survivor reported that the aircraft, after sinking the ship, had repeatedly sprayed those in the water with machine-gun fire.

The sinking of the *Mumutu* and the death of Father Henry Matthews and Leslie Gariadi happened on 7th August 1942, the Feast of the Holy Name, and a day before Father Matthews's chaplaincy was to have expired.

OF NEW BRITAIN

In December 1942 the *Review* of the Australian Board of Missions contained this brief note: "No news has been received of the Reverend John Barge or the Reverend Bernard Moore, both of whom were carrying on their work along the coast of New Britain when the Japanese landed. We have been advised that they have both had opportunities of getting out, but have elected to remain with their native flock."

John Barge was an Englishman, born at Cowley, Buckinghamshire, and educated at Twyford and at St John's Royal Latin School. He served in the First World War from 1915 to 1918 and in 1926 came to Queensland to stay with a sister. He went fruit-farming in the Stanthorpe district for a year or two but, under the influence of Canon W. P. B. Miles of the Charlotte Street Anglican Mission, Brisbane, he worked as an honorary catechist and then entered St Francis's Theological College, Nundah, in 1928. He served his curacy at St James's, Toowoomba, though it was more particularly in St Thomas's, Jellicoe Street, that he worked for the great part of his four years' ministry.

In 1936 when he felt a call to go to the mission field, he was sent first to Rabaul, the head-station of the Melanesian Mission in New Britain. His work was to establish contact with the native boys working in and round the capital of the territory of New Britain. He used the service book of the Melanesian Brothers — the Retatasiu — which the boys found easy to follow. The services were held in the little church house every evening and at St George's Church on Saturdays and Sundays. The boys who came to the well-attended services were chiefly employed around the town as cooks, gardeners, launderers, and labourers. Some of the boys came from technical and public schools and with their education were able to help with the teaching of others. These Christian gatherings exerted a great influence on native boys cut off from their village life, and when their term of service was over, they carried the teaching they had received back to their villages. One of the boys went on to Au mission station on the south coast of New Britain to work with the Reverend G. Voss.

From Rabaul, John Barge went to Malaita in the Solomons, where he had training at the mission hospital so that he might learn about the treatment of tropical complaints. Medical work was to become one of his absorbing interests and the relief of suffering his greatest desire. His next stay was at Maka on Malaita, helping the Reverend J. Edwards in his work of training ordinands for the ministry. While still in the Solomons he had the interesting experiment of working with a group of native teachers brought to the Solomons from New Guinea. The course had to be as simple as possible, for the people of New Britain had not the advantage of a Christian background as many of the Solomon Islanders had.

In April 1939 he was established on the south coast of New Britain, with his headquarters at Iumielo, at one end of the district, and with Urin as a base at the other. The Bishop had placed two "Households" of Melanesian Brothers along the coast and in the Ilak portion of the district, so the work of the Melanesian Mission along the coast of New Britain was already well under way.

The supervision of the work of the double district of Ilak–Moewe* was shared by John Barge with the Reverend Bernard Moore and the group of Melanesian Brothers who had Au as their base. Bernard Moore had in addition the hazardous task of conveying stores and supplies, as well as mail, from Rabaul to the outlying places. He had joined the mission in 1936 and, after serving in the school at Pawa, Ugi Island, and helping with the training of native teachers, he had been ordained and transferred to the Mandated Territory of New Guinea on the south-west coast of New Britain. When the mission vessel, the *Cecil Wilson*, became too unsafe for use on the long trip to Rabaul, he carried on with a smaller vessel, the *Mary Stafford*.

The two priests were great friends, and the short intervals of companionship they shared together helped greatly in giving them confidence and courage to face their lonely lives and to make the decision to remain at their posts when a clear and honourable way to safety was offered them. Though missionaries were given the option of remaining, the advice of the government in December 1941 was that all in isolated places should take whatever transport to safety was available.

After the capture of Rabaul and the Japanese occupation of most of the islands, communication with the missionaries in New

*Now called Pulie–Kandrian.

Britain was cut off and for over a year no word was received about them. Then it was learnt that, as the Japanese forces moved down the coast, Roman Catholic priests who were taking an opportunity to leave had asked John Barge to come with them, but he declined in order to remain with the people. Bernard Moore was also given the chance but, after making contact with John Barge and finding that he was remaining, Bernard Moore made his own decision to stay. After a meeting and a discussion the two friends made their plans to carry on for as long as possible in their respective areas.

The Japanese occupied Gasmata on the south coast and set up a base there. Twice Japanese soldiers visited Kandrian, near John Barge's station, and asked the natives if there were any Europeans in the area, but the people did not betray the missionaries. Peter, a staunch Christian, and the luluai, begged John to come to Apugi with them where they would hide him; but John refused and carried on with his work. He had a well-equipped dispensary and had been deeply grieved by the sufferings caused by yaws and ulcers which eroded great sections of flesh on faces and limbs. His conviction was that the work of healing should go hand in hand with the preaching of the Gospel.

Once the natives persuaded him to visit a cave that they said would completely hide him if the Japanese came again. It was so low that he had to crawl into it. His brief comment was that he would die on his feet if it came to that, but he would not be caught like a rat in a hole.

The silence of eighteen months was broken in June 1943 when the New Guinea office in Australia was able to announce that "John Barge is away back in the hills, and the natives are looking after him". Of Bernard Moore there was no information. It seems that John Barge was able to serve his people for nearly two years of the Japanese occupation, and was working until about two months before the arrival of American forces at Ambut. This would place his capture by the Japanese as in October 1943. By that time Allied forces were putting pressure on the Japanese, who, realizing that their domination of New Britain was seriously challenged, began drastic mopping-up operations.

A Japanese destroyer bent on routing out any remaining Europeans was passing Kandrian, and the mission house at Pomete was sighted. A landing-force went ashore and found John Barge going about his daily work quite openly. Some sort of conversation took place, for the local natives later reported that the Japanese told them they were taking John Barge to Gasmata where he could get some medical supplies and that they would bring him back. The impression given was one of friendliness and no resistance was made.

After rounding the next point the ship turned into Moewe Harbour (which is Kandrian), and John Barge was taken ashore. Two natives and Gordon, brother of the teacher Peter, were hiding in the bush and witnessed the killing of the missionary. He was executed on a track near a village garden, "with shot and sword". The natives ran to tell Peter, who hurried to find "Father, sitting by the side of the track, as though he was resting — but he was dead". They buried him there and marked his grave with a border of coral. In 1947 the Bishop of Melanesia read the burial service over the grave at the spot known as "Vivilo".

The time and manner of the passing of the Reverend Bernard Moore are not known.

Rest eternal grant unto them, O Lord; and let light perpetual shine upon them.

6

The Confessor

THE CELL was a square of deep gloom. One small electric-light bulb, high in the roof, was so placed over the galvanized-iron partition that it cast a little light into a corner of the two adjoining cells; the bulb was draped with a piece of dirty red calico to prevent any light showing outside. Behind me a key turned in the lock; then I heard the click of metal, and saw a pair of handcuffed hands come out from under the net which lay across one corner; a voice whispered something, and the hands made signs for me to come inside the net. So I moved across and peered uncertainly into the corner and saw a small and very weatherbeaten Japanese, about fifty years old. Whispering, he tried to tell me who he was, and why he was there — at least I thought this must be what he was saying, but as his only word of English was "quartermaster" our conversation soon petered out. So I lay down, in the narrow confines of the net, alongside the criminal quartermaster, wondering what was the nature of his crime. And so the night passed, slowly. I remember thinking to myself that Paul and Peter had both been in prison, so had our dear Lord Himself. So I said Compline and reminded myself that "Stone walls do not a prison make, nor iron bars a cage"; prayer is the essential freedom, transcending all locks and bars, all walls and frontiers; I could well understand Paul and Silas singing in their cell. Indeed I determined there and then that I would sing myself, at least once every evening. And I began to chant one of the lovely Compline psalms:

> *Hear me when I call, O God of my righteousness.*
> *Thou hast set me at liberty when I was in trouble:*
> *Have mercy upon me, and hearken unto my prayer.*

I felt very vividly that night the great truth of the Communion of Saints. I remember saying to myself: "Not only are Paul and Silas and Peter here; but all that vast multitude who, down the ages have sung these psalms and said these ancient prayers; so also are those who tonight are saying Compline." I thought of the places where I had said the Office, and of those of my friends who would be saying it now. My last conscious thought was to say the words of the ferial antiphon:

Save us O Lord, while waking; and guard us while sleeping:
That awake we may be with Christ, and in peace may take our rest.

When Father James Benson was separated from Sister Hayman, Mavis Parkinson, and the party of soldiers, he tried to work his way back towards the sound of firing but became hopelessly lost. As he heard the fire of the American soldier's tommy-gun roar out, but farther and farther away in the distance, he made a decision that it was his duty to stand by the Papuan people and that the best thing he could do for them now was to find the Japanese and give himself up. He consoled himself over his separation from the Sisters and the soldiers with the thought that he was the only non-combatant man in the party, the oldest, and probably a terrible liability if he failed to stand up to the journey across the Owen Stanleys.

For five days he wandered without food, his only drink some yellow, brackish water from a waterhole and a little rain he caught in his groundsheet. On the sixth day he struck the Gona road and, putting on his old cassock, set off along it to meet the Japanese Army. Soon he ran into a group of several hundred Japanese soldiers. To his statement, "I am the priest from Gona", the only response was the cry of "Spy!" A Japanese soldier punched him about the face, knocked off his spectacles, kicked him on the shin, and threw away his mosquito net and ground sheet. The officer who had called him a spy, ordered him to carry his rucksack.

Father Benson staggered a few yards before falling under the load. On his knees he wriggled his arms out of the shoulder straps and motioned to the officer to cut off his head with his sword. Then, making the sign of the cross, he commended his soul to God and began to repeat the *Nunc Dimittis* — "Lord, now lettest Thou thy servant depart in peace. . . ."

He had said a couple of sentences when, to his surprise, the officer not beside him, took his head in his hands, turned Father Benson's face to his and, holding him gently by the shoulder, led him to the side of the road to sit down. The officer shouldered his own rucksack and the troops, four-deep, marched past the seated white priest. Then came the guns and ammunition carried by natives. When the line of troops grew thinner, Father Benson wandered along the road towards Buna until he came to the village of Soputa. Some friendly soldiers offered him water and food, and he lay down to sleep beside the corner post of the rest-house.

In the morning, he climbed into the back of a truck heading towards the coast. Some Japanese soldiers piled in, and priest and soldiers (for the Japanese troops were very fond of English songs of the First World War) joined in the singing of "It's a long way to Tipperary", each according to his own version. At Sanananda he was taken to the Military Police camp, where he was questioned by an aggressive sergeant-major whose only comments on his statements were cries of "Spy!" and "Lie!" At night the sergeant-major handcuffed him, tied both arms tightly above the elbows, across his back, and left him to the mosquitoes. Handcuffed by day, tied and handcuffed by night, he spent three days in this manner until Captain Nakayama, the officer-in-charge of the Military Police, returned, and ordered that he should be taken by a party of soldiers to Gona to test the accuracy of his claim to be their missionary priest.

As the military escort neared one of the villages they began to load their rifles. Father Benson inquired if they were going to shoot him there and was told they were ready to attack any natives. "Please do not shoot my brown people," he begged. "The only weapons they have are wooden spears. They will not harm you." At Gona a couple of mission-boys came out at the familiar sound of the priest's whistle, and Benson encouraged friendly relations between them and the Japanese soldiers. The beautiful mission station was in ruins. Thousands of coconut-trees lay uprooted; great bomb craters formed a pattern along the gray sand. Only the Sisters' house, riddled with machine-gun bullets, remained standing.

Next day, Father Benson and the soldiers returned to Sanananda with twenty of the principal men from the Gona district. A conference with Captain Nakayama was conducted with great dignity on both sides, but to the Papuans' plea that their priest

The Reverend Canon Peter Rautamara, who as a boy in 1891 saw the pioneer Anglican missionaries land in Papua, and was the first Papuan to be ordained priest in the Anglican Church.

Bishop George Ambo administers confirmation to a group of Papuan boys. The presenting priest is the Reverend Bevan Meredith.

An assembly at Martyrs Memorial School, Agenehambo.

should be returned to them Nakayama's answer was that until the war ended no white man might go free.

However, he permitted two of the natives to search among the ruins at Gona for any of Father Benson's possessions. Roland Dogi brought him his spare reading-glasses, and one of the teachers gave him his English Prayer Book, which Father Benson retained throughout his captivity. Then by what the priest called "the miraculous incident of the spectacles", a Japanese soldier gave to Roland a pair of old spectacles, with one wing broken and very scratched lens. "Take my glasses to your Father," he said. "They will help him." By a hundred to one chance they were true to sight.

Ten days later Father Benson was seated outside the Military Police tent reading his Prayer Book when an orderly came to take him to Captain Nakayama.

"Benson, you lie," said the captain severely. "Miss Hayman, Miss Parkinson, they are prisoners. You and they fight our soldiers. Okay. Now we have another inquiry; what you call a court martial."

Charged with withholding the information that he had been with a party of enemy soldiers, Father Benson was told that he had placed himself in a serious position and the Japanese military authorities would be justified in taking his life. He replied that to have told the whole story three weeks before would have led to the dispatch of patrols to hunt down the two white women. The sergeant-major tried to lash at him with a round ebony ruler, but Captain Nakayama restrained him. Then the priest went on to tell of the peaceful, active life at Gona, the coming of the Japanese, the flight into the jungle, the meeting with Australian and American soldiers, the attack by the Japanese patrol. He spoke of his six days alone, his finding of the Japanese troops, and of the soldier who said to him, "We fight Americans six days ago. We kill six." It was then that, to help the white women and any survivors, he had decided to make no mention of them. The sergeant-major laid about his head with the ruler, but again Nakayama reached out and caught his hand.

"Captain Nakayama, what would you do in similar circumstances?" asked Father Benson.

Without hesitation, the Japanese replied, "I hope I would do the same."

F

Father Benson bowed and thanked him. Captain Nakayama alone among the Japanese soldiers at Sanananda was a practising Buddhist. Each morning, after careful washing, he would stand on the edge of the forest and, facing the sun, would bow low three times and carry out his devotions for five or six minutes.

Some months elapsed before Father Benson was taken to Rabaul to the prison cell where he spent the next year. On an almost saltless diet he contracted beri-beri, and his legs developed nasty swellings. Boils broke out across his shoulders and arms. Sleep became impossible. Saguro, a Christian interpreter who had been his good friend, tried to wipe the filth from the boils, but an officer called him and subjected him to face-slapping for several minutes. Benson now knew what Saguro had meant when he said that it was hard to be a Christian in the Japanese Army.

On Christmas Day Father Benson said mattins and mass, but instead of the consecration he made an act of spiritual communion. The food for the day was cold, unsalted rice left over by the guards the night before; but still he felt a strange happiness. Towards evening, Saguro came with the message that the captain of the jail wished to speak with him. The captain was standing with his hands behind his back. Then, with Saguro interpreting, the following conversation, recorded by James Benson in *Prisoner's Base and Home Again*, took place:

"Today is Christmas. Christmas for the Christians is a happy day, is that not so?"

"Yes," I replied, "a very happy day."

"And why is Christmas a happy day?"

"Because," I said, "on this day God became man to save us from sin, and to make us His sons."

"Do you really believe that?"

"I don't only believe it. I know it."

"And that is why you are happy?" He sounded puzzled. "But are you really happy?"

"Yes, I am really and deeply happy, because nothing that may happen to my body can prevent my being the child of God. Though perhaps," I could not help adding, "I should be even more happy if my body also were free."

"Yours," said the captain, "is a very beautiful faith; I would like on this day to make you even more happy, so I give you a present."*

He unclasped his hands from behind his back and presented the white prisoner with a half-pound of biscuits and a packet of jellies. These Father Benson, to the disapproval of Saguro, shared with his fellow prisoners.

With the coming of a major of Secret Police (afterwards tried and condemned as a war criminal), life in the jail at Rabaul was changed greatly for the worse. In the cell, fifteen feet square, seventeen men were crowded. Rain poured through the rusty roof and unshuttered window. Two men lost their reason. When some New Britain natives were placed in the cell, Father Benson formed a class on the catechism. Four had been baptized by the Sacred Heart Fathers, but the instruction was in the great Catholic verities of the Christian Church. All in the cell joined in the Lord's Prayer and listened to the Gospels, and then in the soft singing of hymns at evening. The captain and three or four of the Military Police guards would come and listen.

Father Benson was the only white man to see both the arrival of the Japanese Army at Gona and the evacuation of the remnants driven back over the Kokoda Trail. He was in a Japanese transport being taken to Lae when the transport was hove to and, from a mass of makeshift rafts, men were taken aboard so wasted by dysentery and fever that they looked like skeletons. These were, he was told, the only survivors of the Japanese Army that had landed on the coast of Papua. The recapture of the mission station was announced by the Australian commander to his superior, in the laconic phrase: "Gona's gone."

On 25th October 1945 at Christ Church St Laurence, Sydney, Father Benson celebrated the Holy Communion for the first time since that day at Siai when he had celebrated the Mass of St Laurence with May Hayman and Mavis Parkinson. Bishop Philip Strong, who had just given him his second commission and blessed him, acted as his server.

Back at Gona mission station, Father Benson presided at the Easter meeting when the Ogabadas (churchwardens) discussed what should be done with the Easter offerings. Conway Aiga,

*Benson: *Prisoner's Base and Home Again*, pp. 98, 99. By kind permission of the publisher, Robert Hale & Co.

the senior Ogabada, though not an old man, expressed his opinion: "Father and friends, I think God will be happy if we use some of that money to help the Japans who spoilt our country. They are a spoiling people, but if we help them to know and love God, then they will be a helping people. So I think it would be a good thing and pleasing to God if we use half that money to send his Gospel to the Japans and the other half to buy new things in place of those the Japans destroyed."

Another Ogabada stood up and said, "The words of Conway are good words and we shall do them."

Then the people cried, "Awara!" which means "Amen" or "All right".

The people had rebuilt a mission house for their priest. At a meeting held after mass on 6th October 1946, attended by some three hundred men and youths, with the women sitting under trees and on the beach, plans were decided upon for reconstruction of the Church's work at Gona. A temporary church and school were to be opened by January 1947, and plans were made for the erection of a permanent church in memory of May Hayman and Mavis Parkinson.

The thoughts of James Benson at this time may be gathered from the minutes he recorded and the notes he made of this meeting and following meetings of the Gona Public Trust. He was training the people for what he considered to be the best features of a white democracy. The Trust later became the Gona District Co-operative Society. Before the war he had given some instruction about the early development of the co-operative movement in England. The Papuans were dependent on their gardens for food. They were not nomads, nor were they peasant farmers. There was little wildlife, and though mission and government had urged the villagers to plant coconuts, this was no longer dependable as a profitable product. It was becoming clear that some form of economic organization based on their tribal life was urgently needed. "If the European-owned plantation is to be the only form of agricultural production," said the enlightened Administrator, Colonel J. K. Murray, "the native is doomed to remain a hewer of wood and a drawer of water."

For Father Benson, the alternative was for the Church to develop a Christian co-operative movement, and it was in educating the Papuans around Gona in co-operative principles that he spent much of his later life. When the representatives of eight villages gathered at Gona to form their first co-operatives he told them, "The Christian co-operative movement is an integral part of the Papuan Church. From the Christian co-operative will come the first Papuan bishop." One of the speakers at the first meeting of the Gona Public Trust was George Ambo, teacher at Gomberin, fourteen years later to be consecrated first Papuan Bishop.

Father James Benson died in England in 1955. He had gone there partly to learn bootmaking. In his hookworm-infested area he wanted to teach bootmaking to his people, people too poor to buy shoes.

7

The Years After....

WHEN Bishop Strong was permitted to visit the war-torn strip of his diocese in April 1943, his ship for part of the journey was a barge with an outboard motor that had a trick of breaking down when out at sea. Then the Bishop and his companion had to resort to the use of two small oars.

At Dogura and the eastern stations the staff had quietly carried on during the fighting. An A.I.F. lieutenant, arriving at Dogura after weeks spent struggling with his men through the jungle, wrote home:

I was utterly surprised when we reached our destination at the complete transformation of scene — gone were the jungle, rain, and mud — instead we found beautiful grass lands and verdant hills, bathed in glorious sunshine, with native villages strewn along shelving, coconut-palm shores. This is a veritable paradise, and it seems like an oasis after the dark, steamy jungle scene a week ago. I have not seen a happier lot of people than the natives here, and it is a pleasure to observe them, stripped of the conventions which form the bugbear of our white civilization. The girls wear only banana-leaf skirts and rightly so, as it would be a crying shame to conceal more of the bronze beauty of their bodies. All of them have been at the Anglican Mission here and are beautifully clean. Theirs is an ideal unspoilt life, playing in the sun, fishing, tending their gardens. We trade tobacco, biscuits and bully beef with them for fruit and vegetables, but even if we had nothing to offer, they'd overwhelm us with hospitality just the same.

In the northernmost part of the diocese, Mamba mission station, a conspicuous landmark on a hill had become a convenient rendezvous for Japanese bombers from Rabaul and their fighter escorts from Salamaua, when a raid for Port Moresby was preparing. Archdeacon Romney Gill, with the "family of fifty" who held firmly to him, moved from temporary resting-place to temporary resting-place in safety. Mamba station was utterly destroyed. It was the work of a great part of his thirty-four years in Papua, for Romney Gill was a patient and skilful technician. The raids destroyed the dispensary, the hospital where seven thousand treatments a year were given, the elaborate water, telephone and electric lighting systems.

The Bishop arrived at Gona to find the mission station a heap of ashes, but from a mile along the beach could be seen still standing the great station cross. In the late afternoon the Bishop met two boys, one going towards the villages of the north, the other towards the south. They immediately recognized him and came running eagerly. "Go and tell your people that their Bishop is here," said the Bishop, "and that tomorrow morning at 6.30 he will celebrate the sacrament near the station cross."

The area was the most war-devastated settled part of Papua, but the next morning two hundred and fifty Papuans came filing along the tracks, gathering around the cross while two hundred knelt at the spot where the communion rails had been. The native hymns, led by the faithful teachers and their wives, were a sonorous chant of triumph.

From a friendly Australian captain the Bishop recovered two portions of the station log, and he was then driven on in an American truck to Sangara. There many of the surrounding villages sent their whole remaining populations to the requiem which the Bishop celebrated, and then all joined in a procession to the grave of Mavis Parkinson and Sister Hayman. The Bishop conducted the burial service over the grave, but a small boy kept repeating the word "Lucian", and it became clear that the body of Lucian Tapiedi was also there. It had been brought by a faithful Christian from the track near Jewaia Creek and lay separated by a small railing from the grave of the two white women. Another burial service was held, the railing removed, and the three graves enclosed by a fence joining Australians and Papuan.

At Isivita, Andrew Uware came forward to render an account of the stewardship given him by Father Henry Holland. He had, in accordance with the priest's final instructions, given a great part of the mission stores to feed the hungry, but some he had sold. Standing before the improvized altar with a notebook in one hand and a grubby white calico bag in the other, and with the village to bear witness, he handed over the small sum as the foundation amount with which a new mission might be built.

In the ruins of the mission house the Bishop sat down to search through the scraps of paper to see if any of the work of Henry Holland could be rescued. He found a letter written by Bishop Henry Newton during the years of the depression. Henry Holland had sought to expand his work into a new area, but Bishop Newton had had to reply that Holland's grant for future years would be cut down — to £216 per annum. It was in the area that Henry Holland had been debarred from evangelizing that unfriendly natives had delivered the aged missionary, Vivian Redlich, and the others into the hands of the Japanese.

The problems that confronted the Anglican Mission were immense. "Since the beginning of 1941," wrote the Bishop after the war, "we have lost thirty-three missionaries." Eleven had died, most of the others had been defeated by ill-health. There were only four replacements. The *Maclaren King*, taken over by the military, had been lost in action. The war had caused an inflation of prices, and the diocese found its meagre income would go only half as far as before the war. The Administration had tacitly handed over to the Anglican Mission the responsibility for medical work on the northern coast. From Samarai to the border of the Trust Territory of New Guinea there was not a single doctor, and the medical staff consisted of the five nurses of the mission. There was not a single government school.

To the destruction of war was added the devastation from a cyclone and tidal wave that hit the coastal area from Gona to Mambare River. Village after village was swept away. The gardens, which had shown promise of being the most fruitful for years, were totally destroyed. Eight people were drowned. Slowly the work of rebuilding on the shattered foundations continued. Communication was restored when the Secretary of the A.B.M., the Reverend M. A. Warren, took to Papua the *St George*,* a

*After Canon Warren's death in Sydney in 1963, his ashes were committed to the ocean from the *St George* off the Papuan coast by the Bishop of New Guinea.

small motor-cruiser. He then captained the *St George* along the coast from Samarai while the Bishop visited the stations of Menapi, Dogura, Sefoa, Eroro, Dewade and Lae. Visits were made to the army establishments at Oro Bay and to the United States Naval Base at Milne Bay in search of building material the United States Forces might care to make available to the mission.

At Boianai, where he spent Christmas Day, the Bishop found the natives unsettled and perturbed by their life with the army. He encouraged them to return to their villages as soon as possible, to assist the mission in its work, and to co-operate with the Administration.

The medical problem was how to organize the resources of the mission to meet the needs of the whole coastline from Milne Bay to the old German border. Sister Tomkins was at Taupota and Sister Roberts at Wanigela, while at the isolated Mamba station the veteran Archdeacon Romney Gill was both doctor and nurse.

It was decided to concentrate the hospital work at Dogura and at Eroro. With the help of army buildings left at Eroro, Sister Jean Henderson established St Margaret's Hospital. From the start she advanced the revolutionary idea that Papuan girls be trained as nurses. The Papuans told her that nursing was not proper work for their women. Two of her trainees ran off and had New Guinea marriages. One left because the village people made her life unbearable. The village sorcerer terrified a dying patient in her last hours. Yet there were girls who wanted to join as nurses despite the opposition of the village people. Sister Henderson closed the out-patients department and told the village leaders that she refused to attend any cases until she had nurse trainees. Within three days she had four assistants.

To Gona the Bishop dispatched Sister Elliott, just in time to cope with an outbreak of measles. The government proclaimed isolation measures but offered no means to enforce them. The overworked Sisters were greatly cheered by the arrival of Dr Blanche Biggs, who after a few months' work at St Margaret's Hospital set off on patrol work.

Dr Biggs took with her on her patrols a box of medicines and two, three or four boys according to the length of the patrol. Those she regarded as hospital cases she sent to Sister Henderson at Eroro. "Until we have the confidence of the far-distant people," she wrote, "and until the people realize that their sickness needs white man's medicine, village visiting is the best means of getting in touch with them." The problem of the children greatly worried her. "The curse of these children is anaemia," she declared. "It is hard to assess which is the most important of three factors causing it — hookworm infestation, malaria, or poor diet. In most cases, I think, it is the first. It is the little children, up to ten years of age, who are the sufferers. But I estimated that to give iron tonic to all the children who needed it, in two schools, would take four times as much of the raw materials as I have in stock. Iron will be a large item in my next order."

It was not until the end of June 1947 that the Bishop thought it advisable to call in his depleted staff for what should have been an annual conference. At the first conference of the Anglican Mission since 1941, there assembled at Dogura less than half of those present in 1941; but there was no question of retreat. In his Charge the Bishop announced plans for extending what had been in effect a diocese of Papua so that it took over New Britain from Melanesia and the Trust Territory of New Guinea.

On the Feast of St Laurence the Bishop ordained three Papuan deacons to the priesthood, and the aged Bishop Newton, who was to die a few weeks later, was carried in his bed into Dogura Cathedral to assist at the ordination of those he had trained for the ministry and one of whom he had baptized.

Education was the dominant note of the conference, and it was there that the idea arose of a memorial secondary school at Sangara — the Martyrs Memorial School — to which the cream of the students of the mission station schools might be sent for higher education. At the November meeting of the A.B.M. a promise was made of £5,000 towards the building of the school; but the zeal of the Papuan people outstripped the generosity of the grant. By February 1948 the school was opened, blessed and dedicated by the Bishop.

To the A.B.M. Bishop Strong wrote: "The different districts banded together and each made its contribution towards the erection of temporary buildings, some by giving materials, and others by doing the work of erection as well as the general giving of money and gifts to the Martyrs Fund. The Sangara people themselves made a very generous offer of land to the mission and

cleared the land themselves, and it is upon part of this land that
the temporary school has been built."

By European academic standards it was not a very magnificent
secondary school. There were two large classrooms, the office,
workshop and garage of the mission station serving as classrooms
for typing, book-keeping, carpentry and engineering. At the
opening of the school there was a dormitory to accommodate forty
boarders from out-stations and there were thirty Sangara day-
boys. Within a year the numbers had risen to 103 boys and girls,
aged fourteen to eighteen years, of whom 67 were boarders from
Mukawa, Wanigela, Sefoa, Eroro, Gona and Isivita. An addi-
tional dormitory, a refectory and a third large classroom had been
built.

Judged by Australian standards, the burden placed upon the
Martyrs School principal, Miss Margaret Louise de Bibra, B.A.,
Th.L., Dip.Ed., was intolerable. She was without white staff until
the arrival of a trained secondary school teacher, Miss Nancy
White, in July 1948. She had, beside the memorial secondary
school, charge of the Sangara primary school, which with 410
pupils was the largest in the area. In addition to her Papuan
staff she directed the Papuan teachers in charge of out-station
schools, having in this way some two thousand children under
her supervision.

The Reverend David Hand, who was for a time at Sangara as
relieving priest-in-charge, had a very clear idea of the difference
of opinion in the territory between those now ardently advocating
education for the Papuan. There were, he pointed out, plenty in
trade or in government offices who were eager that the mission
should pursue the new objective of secondary education. But what
they wanted were clerks, interpreters, store-boys, "boss-boys".
Their criterion of education was the Papuan's ability to assist the
smooth running of the white man's administrative or money-
making machines. The result would be the "education" of the
Papuan out of his milieu, the separation of the educated from his
people, and the inevitable social consequences of young men being
cut off from the standards of their own people or any other
standards.

The objective of the Anglican Mission was to educate the
Papuan into his own background, with a view to his helping to
raise his own people on their own level. With the approach of

responsible government in Papua–New Guinea it is fair to ask whether the Anglican Mission did not have in those years of intensive white exploitation, 1947-51, a clearer idea of the future needs of a people, almost entirely living by subsistence agriculture in small villages, than did the government of Australia or the traders.

The Administration requested the mission to train a number of young men under the Commonwealth Rehabilitation Scheme. At Dogura by the end of 1949 there were ninety-two men under the supervision of Canon Bodger; a number of them were married and there were seventy-eight dependants. Family houses, each accommodating three families, were built for the married men. The gardens provided crops of potatoes, beans, pumpkin, bananas, etc., and pawpaw trees were flourishing. The Dogura herd of cattle was doing well, and six herds had been built from it to be sent to other places. Land was set apart for stock; rice, maize, sweet potatoes, lucerne and sorghum had done well. A beginning was being made with the care of sheep and poultry. All the work, of course, was being done with secondhand machinery. "This cultivation," reported Canon Bodger, "will result in a saving of rice, besides giving a better and more varied diet." Canon Bodger, a man of infinite capacities, instructed the men in carpentry, simple engineering, animal husbandry and agricultural subjects.

Miss Margaret Devitt and Miss Ena Somerville taught typing, bookkeeping and business principles. In addition, Miss Somerville was resident teacher of the nearby St Agnes's Home for half-caste children. Here, as well as a general education, the children were taught music, sewing, folk dancing, woodwork and gardening. The two white women gave talks on food values, hygiene and mothercraft to the wives of the men sent by the Administration.

The work of training selected Papuan young men as teachers and evangelists was carried out at St Aidan's College under Canon Oliver Brady, who in 1950 had charge of forty-three students, of whom twelve were married. It was upon these young men that the future of a Church of Papua depended. The day began with communion at 6 a.m., exercise in the form of cutting back the ever encroaching jungle from 7 a.m. till 8 a.m., followed by a swim in the surf. Morning prayer was said alternately in English and a native language, then studies until 2.30 p.m. The college language, according to mission tradition, was English, never Pidgin English. "It is just as easy to teach a simple pure English," declared Canon Brady, "and this opens to the native people a range of reading which is otherwise closed to them."

Canon Warren again made his way north with a ship, this time piloting the *Maclaren King II* on her maiden voyage from Brisbane along the Queensland coast. The voyage was a remarkable one, averaging 8½ knots, even when the rough seas of Milne Bay were taken into the reckoning. There was a great scene of rejoicing when the vessel reached Wedau beach below Dogura, and in 1949 the Bishop was writing that the space of time taken by him in the *Maclaren King II* seemed incredibly short.

But it was in the little *St George* that the Bishop went off with the Assistant Bishop-elect, the Reverend David Hand, and a preliminary survey of New Britain. The boundaries of the diocese were being enlarged. Canon Warren and Bishop Hand were exploring the possibilities of establishing fresh mission stations in the highlands of central New Guinea.

In 1950 the Community of the Holy Name made its decision to open a house in the diocese, and at Dogura there was the opening of St Barnabas's Hospital with the objective of training medical orderlies.

On 21st January 1951 Mount Lamington erupted.

8

Mount Lamington

THERE was no word for volcano among the Sangara people. To them Mount Lamington was a friend. There was a tradition of awe among them, but little sense of fear. Writing shortly before the eruption of 1951, a missionary said: "The mount lies behind us and consists of four or five sugar-loaf peaks. We have always loved it for its beauty and nearness. Every morning early on our way across to school from mattins she is there before us, a familiar friend, sometimes so close the trees stood out dark on the shadowed ridge, sometimes blue and sharp, and distant, often swathed with thin scarves of mist. In a short while the clouds would envelop her, perhaps not lifting till evening, when she would rise again, pink-hued at sunset."

The priest-in-charge of Sangara mission after the war was the Reverend Dennis James Taylor. He had joined the New Guinea Mission in 1937, and after a short time at Dogura and Sefoa took charge of Wanigela. Almost blind in one eye, he trained himself to be a first-class New Guinea bushman. In 1942 he guided his wife and young baby and two other women missionaries across the Owen Stanley Range, returning to the Wanigela district where he remained for the greater part of the war.*

When it was necessary for him to seek specialist treatment, he decided to pioneer another route over the mountains, driving in a jeep up the Kokoda Trail as far as Kokoda, then, with carriers from villages en route, he tackled the precipitous climbing, both up and down, of great heights. When Canon Warren visited

*See *Appendix C*. From Wanigela to Abau.

Lae in 1946 in search of a cheap trawler and some launches from the Disposals Commission, he and Father Taylor slept side by side for three weeks amid the army junk heaps at Labu, near Lae, until they succeeded in their quest and set off down the coast with the trawler and its convoy of five small vessels. At Wanigela he had become an experienced navigator, taking launches up and down the coast with great skill. When he came to Sangara he turned to the care of the salvaged jeeps and trucks, which he nursed like children, keeping them continually in commission, driving them along the roughest tracks and through flooded streams. It was the pride of Sangara mission station that, though abandoned government or traders' trucks might frequently be seen lying by the roadside, no one ever saw an abandoned mission truck.

Dennis Taylor had been appointed by the Bishop to restore the missions at Sangara and Isivita destroyed during the Japanese invasion. He was for some time the only priest in the area, and his bushmanship stood him in good stead as he travelled extensively, rallying the native teachers and getting the schools and stations re-established. He organized the re-opening of the mission at Gona and the building of a new mission house in readiness for the return of Father Benson.

At Sangara he built from scrap materials a house that served as a mission house, and when his wife and children were permitted to return to Papua this was their home. His wife, a former teacher, assisted when she could at the Martyrs School.

January 1951 was a quiet month at Sangara. The Martyrs School had passed through its third year; the boarders had been dismissed for the vacation. The principal, Miss de Bibra, had declined to go on holidays, but had taken a few days off to go to Eroro to attend the wedding of Mr and Mrs Rodd Hart and then to Gona to discuss with the teacher-in-charge the possible formation of a Martyrs Memorial School for Girls. On Wednesday, 17th January, she had returned to Sangara where she had gathered together about thirty Papuan teachers for a course of in-service training.

At the neighbouring station of Isivita, five miles from the foot of Mount Lamington, watchers observed smoke emerging from the mountain. On Friday vertical flashes of lightning were seen coming from the peak, and the whole sky seemed alive with electrical activity. On Saturday the village people of the district showed signs of apprehension, and deputations arrived from Pinja, Hamumuta and Popondetta to ask the Reverend Robert Porter, the priest-in-charge, if they might move to the mission station. Permission was readily given, though not all came. When people from several other hamlets asked for permission to come on the station, Father Porter, whose accommodation was taxed to the limit, wrote to the District Commissioner, Mr Cecil Cowley, for advice.

At 4.30 in the afternoon Father Taylor arrived in a jeep from Sangara, bringing with him two of the licensed teachers, George Ambo and Albert Maclaren, who had been attending the in-service course. The two priests discussed what they should do. Father Taylor had been through a volcanic disturbance near Wanigela in 1943. This had been considerably more severe than what was happening at Mount Lamington but had caused no loss of life, only some inconvenience. The priests decided that it was their duty not to set an example of panic but to await official instructions before attempting an evacuation. The experience of missionaries in Papua had caused them not to take an alarmist view of volcanic activity; and Father Taylor could judge only by his own experience and instructions from the District Commissioner.

On the morning of Sunday, 21st January, he read to the people at the family eucharist at Sangara the message he had received from Mr Cowley telling him that he would be given warning if there was any real danger. In all history there have been only four recorded cases of a volcano erupting horizontally. Mount Lamington was the fourth.

At Isivita Father Robert Porter also read to the three hundred who attended the choral eucharist the message he had received from the District Commissioner — there was no cause as yet for alarm. At 10.30 a.m. he was conscious that the rumblings from Mount Lamington had given way to a constant and regular roar which was increasing in volume. He and Sister Pat Durdin, who had come from the hospital, saw a grey mass of thick smoke moving swiftly towards them at ground level. There was only time to pack as many people as possible into the mission house. The people were frightened but orderly, and the priest led them in prayer. The grey mass had been moving so quickly towards the station that Father Porter wondered why the mission house was not enveloped in it. He investigated and found that it had stopped at a point roughly bisecting the mission grounds and that it was being pushed back by a wind that had sprung up suddenly. The line at which the pumice cloud had stopped was clearly marked. It was possible to walk along green grass six yards from the mission house door — and then into thick pumice dust!

The mass of smoke gradually lifted. Father Porter went outside, to be met by dozens of people running forward covered in pumice. Their eyes emerged from completely grey bodies. He ran to Isivita village and urged those there to come to the station. All was now quiet and, as he returned, spots of cold, wet mud fell on his shoulders. Leaving Sister Durdin and Mrs Barbara Lane to look after the sixty or so people in the mission house, he turned to look after a similar number in his own.

There was now a blackness greater than night, relieved only by fierce streaks of lightning followed by deafening bursts of thunder. The people never lost their morale. They knelt in prayer with their priest and he felt a tiny hand reach out for his in the dark. He managed to get a lamp lit, and then went down to the mission house where Sister Durdin was preparing dressings for the first casualties, who were suffering from burns.

At one o'clock the light began to return, though the visibility was not more than a few yards. People with the most terrible burns were now coming into the station. Father Porter gathered all the uninjured or slightly injured into the church and urged them to make their way as quickly as possible to villages farther away. The Isivita teacher, Simon Panderi, and two other Christians, Eric and Kingsford, said they would remain with the white staff.

Father Porter then returned to the agony in the mission house. Some of the victims had almost all their skin burnt off, and their cries were pitiful. The best that could be done was to make dressings from lint and vaseline and apply them to the charred bodies. Sister Durdin was busy administering morphia to the worst cases.

In the afternoon the four men faced the task of digging the first large grave. The roof of the mission House had at least four inches of sand and pumice upon it; Father Porter realized that it would not stand the weight of another fall, and that it had to be cleared as soon as possible. Throughout the afternoon there was constant

G

rumbling, and it was feared that the volcano would erupt again. The dead were placed in the grave but it was not covered in. At evening, the missionaries said evensong together. In the house the dead were moved, but had to be kept inside as a precaution against dogs and pigs outside. Morphia made peaceful the end of those whose chance of life was hopeless. At 9.30 p.m. the constant and regular roar began again, much louder than in the morning; then pumice, sand and large stones began falling on the sorely tried roof. The noise was deafening, and then occurred an explosion that was heard two hundred and fifty miles away. The missionaries, unable to do anything further in the appalling darkness and convinced that the end had come, "sat it out" under the slender protection of the table, talking quietly and praying. It seemed as though the roof could not possibly sustain the weight hurled upon it, but after about an hour and a half the showers of rocks subsided, and the missionaries continued during the night to minister to the injured and dying.

Eighteen people died in the mission house during the night. In the morning Father Porter and the Papuans carried into the church the charred bodies, from which the flesh came away in their hands. While one boy took turns to keep watch, the priest and the others set to work to dig a large grave. Father Porter went to Isivita to get other digging tools and found no one there except a poor imbecile girl sitting under what remained of a house nursing a pig.

Evacuation of the mission now seemed to be the only course. To the amazement of the priest the jeep, covered with rocks and pumice, started. After a reverent though hasty burial service, the mission party set out for Waseta, most of the surviving burn cases being able to walk. Albert Maclaren, who had taken his family to Waseta on the Sunday with the uninjured villagers, had come back early on Monday morning and went before the jeep clearing the path of fallen trees and rocks.

At 12.30 p.m. on the Sunday of the eruption Father Dennis Taylor, in a dying condition, staggered into Monge, an out-station four or five miles from Sangara, which he himself had pioneered. The reconstruction of what happened at Sangara between the morning eucharist and the fatal eruption is based partly on the Bishop's knowledge of the Sangara mission routine for Sunday.

It would seem that Mrs Taylor had gone down to the church about 10 a.m. for the usual meeting with the women, taking with her the baby and second youngest child, leaving the other two at the house at the top of the hill with their Papuan nurse. Father Taylor would either have been at the church himself or gone there when the eruption began. It would have been impossible to climb up the hill back to the house, so he led his wife and two children through the coffee plantation which was a way out of the station. Unable to get them across the rivers he went on to get help.

Then occurred the fatal blast that killed all life in the area. He would have been near the fringe of the cloud of pumice. Terribly burnt, he pushed on until he was found by natives. Seeing he was dying, they were carrying him into the Church of All Saints, Monge, when Mr Rodd Hart met them. Father Taylor was able to explain where he left his wife and children but realized from his own terrible experience that there was little hope that any who went in search of them would come out alive. He was taken by truck to Popondetta, where he insisted on walking into the house where Mrs Hart was staying. He died at 3.30 a.m. on Monday. It was not possible to give any medical aid to relieve his suffering, but he uttered no words of complaint, merely words of apology for causing trouble and frequent inquiry if there were any news of his wife.

From Gona, Sister Nancy Elliott was walking twenty miles through the night. She arrived just as Father Dennis Taylor died. In the early morning Father Benson also arrived from Gona and made the coffin for the body. It was carried from Cape Killerton along the beach to Gona, where it was buried at 4 p.m. beneath the Gona cross — the cross that survived the war.

The eruption that swept away the Martyrs Memorial School took the life of its principal. The body of Margaret de Bibra was found lying near the graves of Mavis Parkinson, May Hayman and Lucian Tapiedi, and was buried beside them. Of the four thousand Sangara people living about the foot of the mountain, there were but four hundred survivors. At the government station at Higaturu perished the District Commissioner, Mr Cecil Cowley, with his son; Dr Martin with his wife and child; Richard Humphries, a close friend of the mission for many years. The District Commissioner had himself been baptized and confirmed by Bishop Newton. The death-roll of white and Papuan workers was of men and women who had worked in harmony with similar principles and ideals.

The loss of Papuan mission workers could not have been more severe. Buried alongside Miss de Bibra was the Reverend John Rautamara, son of the Reverend Peter Rautamara, and considered by the Bishop to be the most outstanding of Papuan clergy. He had worked for some years as a teacher at Sangara before he was ordained, and the whole of his ministry had been spent at Sangara. Although his own language was Wedauan he seemed to have a special vocation for the Orakaiva people, and even to those who did not know the dialect, his preaching seemed to be inspired.

Apart from the teachers gathered for the in-service course, there were the teachers serving in different districts who were on holiday in nearby Sangara villages. Thirty licensed Papuan mission workers died, including eighteen St Aidan's trained men, and also the district teachers and village evangelists who died in their villages. Around Sangara and Isivita was an area that had grown most responsive to the mission since the war. The people had never forgotten the execution of their priests, Henry Holland and Vivian Redlich, and of their Sisters, Nurse Brenchley and Lilla Lashmar.

Here were some of the finest products of the mission's teaching — Ambrose, Arnold, Alban and Jerome of Gona, Barnabas and Roger of Eroro, Augustus, one of the spiritual children of Henry Holland. There was the loyal Jerry of Sangara who, on meeting the Bishop, said of those who had died in an epidemic, "If Sister Brenchley had been here, they would not have died."

There were the solid and devoted teachers, Didymus and his wife and family, Jonathan and Kingsley with their wives and families, Russell and his son and daughter, and Noel, Aaron, Edgar, David and Kingston. There were many hundreds of devout Christians and communicants, the two to three hundred children of St James' School, the many hundreds from the out-stations.

From the surrounding stations, mission workers and officers of the Administration converged on the devastated area. From Eroro came Father John Anderson with Sister Jean Henderson and Dr Gunther, the Director of Public Health. Mr Rodd Hart, after finding Father Taylor, pushed on with Papuan helpers

through villages thick with dead and dying. Those who were
suffering were brought on trucks to Popondetta or down to the
coast where Father Benson, who had walked from Gona,
ministered to them. At Popondetta, Sister Durdin (who scarcely
rested for days), Sisters Henderson and Nancy Elliott (with the
help of their trained medical boys) and the government doctors
prepared cases for flight on the rescue planes which had flown
in from Lae and Port Moresby.

The Reverend W. E. Moren, flying from Lae, brought with
him Paul Rautamara, brother of Father John Rautamara, and
they were the first to enter the Sangara mission after the eruption.
Father Moren gave burial to Margaret de Bibra, two of the Taylor
children, Father John Rautamara, then to the district Commissioner and others at Higaturu before returning to care for the
wounded being sent to hospital in Lae. His visit to Sangara was
followed by that of the Administrator, Colonel Murray, who took
with him the Reverend John Anderson. At the Administrator's
request the priest held a general memorial service at one of the
villages for those now being buried and for those whose bodies
could not be found. He then immediately assisted the Roman
Catholic priest in a requiem mass.

The Bishop of New Guinea, travelling by night and day from
Dogura in the *St George* with Sister Rawlings, arrived at Cape
Killerton to find the beach from there to Gona thick with evacuees
camped in temporary shelters. A thousand people gathered at the
eucharist celebrated at Holy Cross, Gona, of whom seven hundred
received the sacrament. That evening, at the Administrator's
request, the Bishop conducted evensong, which was attended by
Colonel Murray and government officials.

At Wairope, twenty miles from Kokoda, was the largest of the
evacuee camps, with some four thousand people. There Father
Porter had gone, followed, at the suggestion of the Bishop, by all
of the educational staff of the district who could be spared: George
Ambo, the Harts, Albert Maclaren, and Papuan teachers who had
survived the disaster. The mission's educational equipment was
destroyed, but the Administrator arranged for some to be sent
from Port Moresby and dropped by air. The first camp site at
Wairope had to be abandoned. All the rivers in the Mount
Lamington district were playing queer tricks. So much ash and
pumice was washed down the river beds that their level was

raised many feet above normal. The ground where the first camp was established was soon washed away. A new site was chosen at Ilimo, four miles upstream and on high ground. Here a model village was planned, and soon large permanent houses were under construction. With something to do the people were more contented, and soon Albert Maclaren, a four-year trained teacher from St Aidan's, had a school going for three hundred children.*

In 1955 the Reverend Robert Porter, now Bishop Assistant in Ballarat, Sister Pat Durdin, now Sister Patience of the Community of the Holy Name, and Mrs Barbara Lane were awarded the O.B.E. for their services during the eruption.

---

*In a section of the Australian press reports showed the prejudice of these years. It was stated that the mission stations were looted. There was little to loot and that little was left undisturbed. It was also said that the missionaries had told the Papuans that Mount Lamington would erupt if they did not wear shorts. The statement showed a complete ignorance of the teachings of the Anglican Mission on the north coast and of the native wear of Papuan men and women at work, at play, or in attendance at church.

9

"Not Merely from Us . . . but it is from God. . . ."

ARCHDEACON Stephen Romney Gill was in England when the Mount Lamington disaster occurred. A third-generation missionary he served in Papua for forty-four years. In 1938 he was appointed Archdeacon of the Mamba district, and for a salary of £25 a year (and an old sewing-machine to make his clothes) he became the leader — and Christian servant — of four thousand people. Romney Gill was doctor for the Mambare River area, dentist, church-builder. He would turn from constructing a wharf or a lighting plant to devising his famous cigarette-lighter — about the size of a paint-burner. When the Japanese occupied his mission station, his people carried him off with cigarette-lighter and drums of petrol, and an old typewriter so that he could finish his translation of the liturgy into Wedauan.

The Japanese became accustomed to the mission station and began to venture along the jungle paths. Romney Gill moved elsewhere. His first base had been only a few hundred yards from the compound where the Japanese were camped. He had four bases in all, moving at length forty miles up the Mambare River into the jungle until the Japanese withdrew. After the war he established a new headquarters at Dewade and by dint of "scrounging" managed to equip his mission with telephones so that he could be in his office and be able to ring up the hospital, the school or the workshop.

While he was in England he heard from his people. Their chief had suddenly died. They were afraid Father Romney Gill might not be coming back. "Oh dear Father Gill," they wrote, "this request is not from us the Manau boys merely, but it is from God we are speaking. You landed a long time ago on our shore, you brought the news of the Lord Jesus, and our fathers rose up and loved you, and you loved our fathers. Now seeing your sickness our hearts are very troubled. But what does the doctor say? Listening to him, will you return or will you not return?"

For twelve years Romney Gill had been at work on his production of an altar book in Wedauan. It comprised a revised translation of the liturgy, together with those prayers and devotions that from earliest times have been precious to the Church. During the years of hiding he had gone steadily on with it in one temporary "resting-place" after another until it was completed. In 1944 it was hoped that the translation might be printed, but though some £50 was collected it was not possible to go ahead because of postwar problems. While Romney Gill was in England in 1951, he found a firm, Eaton Press of Liverpool, which was willing to undertake the task. By a great effort the firm set up the whole work and submitted page proofs within six weeks.

The thought of returning with his great work accomplished and the appeal from his people were too strong for any medical opinion to overrule. He set off for Papua and on his return to the Mamba district was elected chief of the tribe. No other white man had ever before been so honoured. Stephen Romney Gill served the Mamba people for two more years, then he retired to die soon afterwards on 26th March 1954. He was seventy-six years old.

That appeal to Romney Gill — "Not from us the Manau boys merely but it is from God" — spurred the Anglican Mission under its Bishop to greater efforts after the setback from Mount Lamington. The cream of its Papuan young men had died, the teachers from St Aidan's College it had hoped shortly to admit to the diaconate. The conference in August 1951 at Dogura was subdued, but the keynote was of consolidation and advance into new territories. The delegates were greatly cheered by the kindly visit of the staunchly evangelical Dr Howard Mowll, Archbishop of Sydney and Primate of Australia. It was the first visit of a Primate to the mission to which Albert Maclaren had been commissioned by a former Archbishop of Sydney and Primate sixty years before.

Archbishop Mowll conducted a quiet day for delegates to the conference. He visited the grave of Margaret de Bibra at Sangara, already being covered by the jungle's advance. He was present at

evensong on the spot where the two Sisters from Gona had ended
their lives. On his return to Sydney he spoke at the Chapter House
of his admiration for the New Guinea Mission and its Bishop, and
made a special visit to Christ Church St Laurence. Then he
found time to trace the relatives of missionaries serving in New
Guinea and to tell of their welfare.

At Siai, where the people had made a refuge for Father Benson,
Mavis Parkinson and May Hayman in the jungle, and where
Father Benson had celebrated their last communion together, the
"Church of the Aeka" was born. Rodd Hart took the ageing
Canon Benson by jeep to Divinikovari, leaving him only a ten-mile
walk, which he managed in two days. Father Lester Raurela, who
had ministered to the people in these distant places, other priests,
nurses and Papuan teachers came the old hard way through all the
villages from Gona and via the Amboga swamps.

The beginnings of the Church at Siai dated back to some thirty
years before, when an aged Christian couple, baptized by Copland
King, had come there from the Mamba district. In 1938 Father
Benson had organized the establishment of the Siai mission station,
with sixty-four men and women from Gona carrying altar and
furniture, school gear and blackboards, cupboards and dispensary
furniture, cases of drugs. The Amboga and Kumusi had both
flooded, and the whole area through which the pioneers travelled
was under water, sometimes up to their necks. Where it went over
their heads they had cut down trees and slithered across on them.
Yet only one case was lost.

Throughout the years of war the people had remained faithful,
though many had died. Now the station was a beautiful place with
a bright lawn of green fringed by church, school, houses. There
were 291 catechumens housed in green booths — just a roof of
leaves — waiting for their baptism and the service of confirmation
by Bishop David Hand. There were old sorcerers and cannibals
of former days — some thirty of them — young school boys and
girls, and some who were not yet "hearers".

For a fortnight the final instruction went on, the interviews, the
recitation of the Creed and the Lord's Prayer in the Binandere
language by children to their parents, who marvelled at reading
as one of the great wonders. Then

. . . the procession went to the place of baptism — thurifer, crucifer and taperers, teachers, clergy and the Bishop in cope and mitre, with Andrew Uware and Stanley Tago in attendance. There followed the tiny group of local Christians. All non-Christians were across the creek and lining its banks row on row, with the tangled jungle, ancient, dark and sinister, behind them — symbol of the spiritual darkness and fear from which they were emerging in a still sorcery-ridden country.

The Bishop down at the water's edge took the service as far as the promises and vows. These were administered by one of the priests. Blessing and censing of the waters was by the Bishop, who then returned up the steps with his attendants to receive the new Christians on the bank as they came out of the waters. They made a dramatic group against the wild skyline of flying clouds.

Father John Wardman and Father Lester Raurela, in girdled alb, amice and stole, entered the waters, and, standing in the midst, began to baptize as the double line moved across. Married couples were first — husbands and wives being baptized at the same time. The reverent demeanour of these gentle people, as the holy waters were poured and the sacred words were spoken, was evidence indeed of the mighty power of God, and the New Birth unto righteousness. Then, having passed through the waters, and having put on the white robe of a new life [a clean loin-cloth] they ascended the hill to be received into the Kingdom of God. . . . Signed with the sign of the cross they took their place in line behind the cross, rank on rank, the 291 of them. So when after two hours all were baptized, and the heathen still stood wondering, the glad procession formed up again, and, singing lustily if not exactly tunefully "At the Name of Jesus" in Bindandere, we swung joyfully across the green sward and into the open church.

The following day Bishop David Hand spoke of the tribal customs, of when a boy grows to manhood and is initiated into full membership of the tribe; and the service of confirmation proceeded its ancient liturgical way of prayer and blessing, the unction of oils, the imposition of hands, and the blow on the cheek (to suffer hardships for Jesus' sake).

Bishop David Hand went on to the Daga country, which had been pioneered by the Reverend N. E. G. Cruttwell. The valleys lie inland from Gaiawanaki in Goodenough Bay, and via a long, tedious track to Kanasuru, 2,500 feet above the sea, where the party was continually drenched by the tropical downpour, Then came a climb down into the Kutu gorge, a thousand feet below, then across roaring creeks, up another thousand-foot climb, another drop, and another climb, and then through a pass into the Daga country. There was spread like a crumpled table-cloth the "Shangri-la" of Father Cruttwell. The Bishop knelt and said a Gloria before they plunged down to the neat little village, where the whole population was waiting in two rows with a triumphal arch of palm leaves.

Five hundred voices gave a shout of "Kaiwa-Kaiwa! Kaiawa-Kaiawa!" and then the tribesmen knelt for the Bishop's blessing. Fabian Paisawa, a talented teacher, took the party on to Uni, where there was a certain "Gwatgage" or holy stone, fourteen feet across, rising to a small eminence at one corner. It had been the meeting-place of the tribe in earlier times and it was there that the chief would stand and beat his drum to call the elders, who would sit on the stone, placing their lime-pots in depressions in the stone while the chief, standing on the highest point, would address them in council. The stone had long been neglected and covered with kunai grass and bushes.

Bishop Hand asked the people to clear away the growth and clean up the stone, and when he returned a few days later after visiting the villages of Modeni and Ilaki he ascended the stone, wearing cope and mitre, sprinkled it with holy water and pronounced the words of benediction. In the manner of the early Church, the Anglican Mission built on the foundations of a more primitive belief. The Bishop told the people the story of the Man of Rock, St Peter, and said that the mission to be built on that stone would be the Mission of St Peter.

Father Amos Ganasa, a chieftain by hereditary right, told the delegates at the Jubilee Conference in Dogura that sorcery, its fear and practice, were great enemies of the Church in Papua. Some delegates were inclined to believe that the methods used by the sorcerers were mainly psychological; but others knew, as did Father Amos, that poison was often administered while the victim was asleep.

Father Amos went through the villages he knew to be under the sway of a certain sorcerer and entered the socerer's house. The interview that followed was one in which the sorcerer was at a disadvantage. He was sick with fever and passed soon into an apologetic and contrite state of mind. Father Amos gathered together the faithful teachers and Christians and, following a roughly made cross, the procession wound its way through the nearby villages. There was a great gathering of the people from all these villages, and one of the leading chiefs addressed them.

"My father," he said, "was a big sorcerer and killed many people, and now I have taken his place. Today, I saw this is wrong and I will destroy all my things and see that all my people give up this bad custom."

The gathering voted against the age-old practice of sorcery and decided (probably to the regret of anthropologists) to burn all the apparatus of sorcery, the magic leaves, sticks, strings and pots with which charms were woven and poisons prepared. Such as could not be burnt were handed over to authorized Christians to be kept for a decision by the Bishop.

A newer pattern of mission work became defined when the Bishop received from the Episcopal Church of the United States a Cessna 170 aeroplane capable of carrying four passengers and their baggage. The aeroplane was to be stationed near Eroro to allow the Bishop swifter travel to northern stations and to enable the transport of urgent cases from the outer stations to St Margaret's Hospital.

At Embi, on a site of fifty-two acres, a tuberculosis hospital was established with three hundred beds, something beyond the wildest dreams of Dr Blanche Biggs. St Luke's, Embi, which later was to house both tuberculosis and leper patients, was financed by the Administration but staffed and controlled by the diocese. Today, with the battle against tuberculosis and leprosy being won, the hospital is assisting in the work of malaria control.

At Dogura Canon Brady with an average of fifty-odd teacher trainees each year decided that students should go from St Aidan's in their fourth year to receive teaching practice and instruction in method at St Paul's, which should rank as a teachers' training school. In 1955 the native people of Papua for the first time took part in the councils of the Anglican Church in Australia when John Guise and Laurence Modudula represented their diocese at General Synod sitting in Sydney.

But other changes were coming to the once isolated posts of the New Guinea Mission. At Wanigela, immediately alongside the mission station, the Commonwealth Scientific and Industrial Research Organization established a research centre, and to Wanigela, as to other places, came a new generation of white settlers from Australia.

10

Self-support for the Papuans

AT A TIME when self-government for New Guinea had not even been discussed in the Assembly of the United Nations and when Australian governmental policy was obsessed with the ambition to exploit its colonial possessions, the Anglican Mission was struggling to implement its belief of "Self-Support for the Papuans". Money was never available, staff was never adequate, in numbers or training, equipment was primitive and secondhand. But in the light of present-day New Guinea it may be claimed that the mission had in the years after the war until the appointment of Paul Hasluck as Minister for Territories a clearer notion of the long-distance needs of the Papuan people than did many of the young officers of the Administration, or those preoccupied with exploitation of the country's resources.

Early in 1950, preaching before the Governor-General of Australia in St John's Church, Port Moresby, Bishop Philip Strong stated the case for close co-operation between missions and Administration, the tradition held by Sir William MacGregor, Sir Hubert Murray and Colonel J. K. Murray:

This territory has been, up to the present, contaminated less than any other native land with the worst features of our civilization, though some of these have been increasingly finding their way into native life in the last decade. The main policies of the Civil Administration of Papua–New Guinea, especially in its object of the uplift of the native peoples, are Christian in spirit and sense. And it must be squarely faced that much opposition to them is not Christian, but is based on self-interest and sometimes even on racial prejudice. . . . This territory from its earliest days has been blest with having many white settlers who have not only been humane but brotherly in their dealing with the native peoples. Not all, of course, have been so, but in the main it has been so and we must see that it continues to be so.

A month later Canon John Bodger was writing very bluntly from Dogura about the problems created by the demand for labour made by the incoming white settlers: "We hope to train mechanical farmers and that is the future for this part of the territory if the people are going to survive. From a local village 60 per cent of the able-bodied men are away in the towns of Port Moresby, Samarai, etc., while their children get hardly enough to keep them alive. I am writing a circular letter to the firms and to the Administration on the matter, stating that unless they see to it that their employees send a certain amount of their wages (which are high) either in cash or kind to feed their relatives, I shall do all in my power to dissuade them from working away from home."

The position in Port Moresby, which lay outside the mission area allotted to the Anglican Church, had earlier been described by Bishop G. H. Cranswick, when Chairman of the A.B.M. He was discussing press opposition to plans for a model village: "This village is part of the Port Moresby settlement. I passed through it a number of times. What our press never said is this. This particular community of Papuan people had to be forcibly dispossessed of their old village during the war. They have now returned to their present site. It is nothing less than a group of hovels, dirty and dangerous in relation to disease. The present conditions, right on the boundary of the capital of Papua, are a disgrace to Port Moresby and Australia."

The building of homes, wharves and great department stores, the influx of officials and their families, of trading concerns and their staffs, meant that scattered outside Port Moresby there were thousands of native people brought there to work, and soon having no intention of returning to their villages. Labour gangs came from the highlands and were used on the waterfront, loading or unloading the ships or working for the petroleum companies. Many were employed as house servants; others worked in the stores and offices or in trades. The housing and accommodation of these native people were being attended to neither by the government nor by private firms. "We find them living together in conditions, sometimes appoaching squalor. With some, money and time in which to be idle lead to many kinds of deterioration. The work of the mission in giving these people a Christian culture can be overthrown within a few months."

This was the opinion of the rector of St John's, Port Moresby, who was placed in a difficult position. Officially, he was there to tend the white population of the town — when they attended his church. Responsibility for the natives in the area lay with other missions. It was impossible to sort out the Papuans who had come from the north coast. Yet the diocese could not stand aside and not do something "to act as a cushion to soften the reaction when natives were hit with a new life". At Koke, just outside Port Moresby, was a market centre for the sale of fish and produce brought by canoes from farther down the coast. Hundreds of natives congregated there each evening, and at the week-end it was crowded. It was surrounded by the so-called living quarters of natives working for the various firms. There the Church established a centre on a small grant of land from the Administration. Natives, who received as little as £1 a week and seldom more than £3 a week, were willing to contribute 2s. to 4s. a week for the maintenance of the centre. A night school was established, and a day school for the children of the workers. Services were conducted as far as possible in the languages of the various peoples.

On the stations of the north coast there were missionaries with a vision, men such as James Benson, David Hand, John Bodger, Dennis Taylor, Alf Clint, Rodd Hart, and Verco Cook. They sought to develop the Papuan people along lines akin to their own tribal customs and as a sovereign, self-supporting people, not as cheap labour. The Bishop of Newcastle, Dr de Witt Batty, was concerned after his visit in 1953 with the feverish white preoccupation with timber exploitation, mining activities, coffee plantations, oil research. He wrote: "I found myself wondering why it should be necessary to draw people such as these, who already enjoy all the facilities for an idyllic existence, into the complexities of our economic system, with all the possibilities of unhappiness which that system involves."

The Papuan social and economic system was based largely on

the Kimta, that loose form of guild for mutual assistance which arose when boys and girls were initiated at the same time, and which lasted for the rest of their lives. A man building a house or making a new canoe could depend upon the members of his Kimta to help with the heavy work. The girls would receive help from their fellow members in times of sickness, childbirth and death. There would be much co-operative gardening and fishing. Before the war James Benson had talked of the foundations of the English co-operative movement to the people around Gona. During the war the co-operative idea was talked about in camps of the Papuan Infantry Battalion and in the labour lines. The readiness to accept co-operatives was almost spontaneous. In 1947 the Joint Mission Conference, which included the Roman Catholic, Anglican, Methodist Churches and the London Missionary Society, endorsed the principles of co-operative formation as a way of developing native economy and asked the government to assist.

The first practical steps were taken around Gona, where the Reverend W. A. Clint, who had been asked by his friend James Benson to come to New Guinea, organized a group of eight village co-operatives; these later grew to fifteen villager producer societies.

Bishop David Hand summed up the significance of the movement thus: "Nothing has been able to stop it because the native people see in it the germ of their own independence, the use of their own land, and there is behind it though not clearly expressed, the feeling of nationalism. Nationalism will rise one day in Papua–New Guinea, and what we do now will determine how we are treated when that comes."

The prevailing white attitude to the co-operative movement was critical and destructive. Private shipping firms refused to carry goods from New South Wales to the co-operatives on the north coast. Papuan co-operative leaders were jailed for not keeping their funds intact, owing entirely to a failure in supervision and not to any wilful misuse of funds. When the first co-operative rice crop was harvested, the Gona people had been unable to get a huller because of the shipping ban. They formed a human rampart round the crop at night against the hordes of rats, at the risk of having toes and fingers eaten by the rats.

The Papuan co-operative movement suffered three crippling

blows in the death of James Benson, the tropical illness of Alf Clint which prevented him from ever returning to Papua, and the enforced resignation of the sympathetic Administrator, Colonel Murray. Colonel Murray had written, "The Administration has welcomed these signs of expanding ambition and has done its utmost to assist the development of native co-operatives." Neither the Commonwealth government at the middle of the century nor many of the officers of the Administration extended the same sympathy and support.

A more understanding attitude was adopted by Paul Hasluck when he succeeded Percy Spender as Minister for Territories. He announced that it was his intention to be right behind the co-operative movement, to set up a special department to deal with the work, and to make officers available to assist any group anxious to start a co-operative.

When Bishop Philip Strong was paying tribute to James Benson in 1955 as the greatest missionary New Guinea had known, he added that one of Canon Benson's achievements was little heard about. There were then 198 registered co-operatives in Papua–New Guinea, and although the work was now supervised by the government, the whole of it was due to James Benson's inspiration and his registration of the first Papuan co-operative. It was he who invited Father Clint to come to Gona and form the foundation co-operatives.*

The Australian Aborigines are a landless people. In Papua–New Guinea, 97 per cent of the country's land still belongs to the indigenous people, although the alienated land includes some of the best and most accessible. Members of the Anglican Mission were conscious of the injustice of some of this alienation. Writing after the Mount Lamington eruption, Bishop Hand commented: "It remains to be seen what the Lands Commission will decide about the Sangara timber lands, but the fact remains that the Sangara people (what remains of them) are very keen to get the lands back; and considering how much they have lost, you would think that any decent-minded government would give the lands

*By 1966 there were 301 co-operative societies with a membership of 97,716, a total capital of $1,821,954 and a turnover of $4,688,424. Secondary organizations numbered 14, with 242 member societies, a capital of $623,011, and a turnover of $1,306,471. *Reports for Territories of Papua and New Guinea, 1965–66.*

back out of hand. . . . The point is that these lands were taken from the people at a stage in their history where they were sufficiently ignorant to be entirely unable to refuse to sell them."

Why, asked the Bishop, does land on cessation of leases revert to the government and not to the original native owners? He pleaded to the government for land for the Sangara people — a great part of the Mount Lamington area had now been barred to them, in addition to that destroyed by the eruption — and was told they might receive two thousand acres. "But I told them not to be content, but to ask for another two thousand acres, so that they can get some lumbering of their own under way co-operatively."

The simple mind of James Benson saw through the speciousness of the arguments used to advance the Pilot Scheme of soldier settlement to be undertaken in the Sangara district. In a letter to a friend in Australia he wrote:

Of course I had a meeting of the people. Rather I just talked to them about it as they sat in their places after the thanksgiving on Sunday. It was still raining. I told the arguments used for soldier settlement: "That they had fought to save New Guinea, etc., they wanted land, etc!" Then I said, "The Papuan Infantry Battalion had fought and died to save Australia, etc. All right then I say, Let the Papuan Infantry Battalion boys go and take up land in Australia."

After all there is more land in Australia than New Guinea, and land is the most precious thing man has next to liberty — indeed he cannot have the liberty apart from the land "That the Lord thy God giveth thee". So I said whatever government or white man comes here *don't sell your land. Do not sell your land!!* You can't get it back and you will then be a slave just working for wages, food and sleep. Of course they Awara! and I am sure they mean it. But I went on to remind them that *they must show the white man that they intend to make as full use as possible of their lands.* . . .

Canon John Bodger and Father Dennis Taylor were both concerned with teaching the Papuan to make full use of his land. For generations the Papuan had been a gardener, dependent upon his small garden for a subsistence living. It was necessary that he should be taught to farm rice, to grow copra for export, coffee and cocoa. The only alternative for many was that they should leave their villages and go to work in the larger towns or on the white plantations. Improved medical care had meant that there was also a higher population in the villages. The death-rate was decreasing, and a greater number of babies was being saved through the work of the baby clinics.

At Jegarata Father Taylor had established before his death a farm for the growing of vegetables. Verco Cook came there, a trained agriculturist intent on showing the people improved farming methods. With his apprentices he cut away the kunai grass and prepared the soil with such tools as he was able to get from Dogura — a little old tractor and some ploughs. The first cereal crop after three years of slow work was ten tons of rice.

With four of the apprentices Verco Cook went to Mekeo on the south coast to learn there the problems of variety and culture, the methods of mechanical harvesting. From the hundred or so varieties selected for experimentation at Jegarata one was found that overcame the difficulty of "lodging" — or collapsing of the unripe crop. This was the greatest impediment to rice-growing in Papua. By 1955 the worst difficulties were being overcome. The huller in the barn was no longer idle. Village rice was coming forward in small, but regular, lots. A step forward had been taken in the policy of self-support — for the Papuan and the Church in Papua alike.

Then tragedy befell the project when the rice crop was hit by a disease, rice-growing in the area was condemned, and a project that had promised to provide the whole of the mission's needs in rice had to be abandoned.

e Mission Cross at Gona, which shows on the cross-arm the holes of Japanese bullets. The cross at the foot stands at the head of the grave of the Reverend Dennis Taylor.

e altar erected in 1968 on the spot near Popondetta where two Australian missionaries, y Hayman and Mavis Parkinson, were put to death by Japanese soldiers in August 1942.

The school day begins with prayers. The Reverend Canon Peter Robin with staff and childr *at Koinambe in the New Guinea highlands.*

The mission station at Koinambe, showing the staff houses, chapel, school and the dispense *grouped around the deba-deba (playing-field).*

I I

"Inasmuch as Ye Did It. . . ."

IN 1939, when the government allotted £22,201 for medical services for the whole of Papua–New Guinea, that hardy missionary on Mamba station, Romney Gill, was wont to regard his dispensary as a workshop where a broken arm might be treated with the same nonchalance — and care — as the repair of any article of mission machinery.

During the fighting from Kokoda down to Sanananda, Buna and Gona, the Australian Army suffered 29,101 casualties from tropical diseases as against 6,154 casualties in battle. Yet when peace came, the Administration was still obliged through lack of staff to let the Anglican Mission carry the whole burden of medical care on the north coast from Samarai to the border of the Trust Territory of New Guinea.

The image of Sister Brenchley escorting her seriously ill cases borne by carriers from Sangara to Gona may today be transformed into that of Sister Pat Durdin in a derelict jeep salvaged from the wreckage of United States Army vehicles; but the responsibility remains the same. When Bishop Strong's Cessna arrived, it was promptly christened *St Gabriel* and, piloted by Bob Hay or his wife, Sister Betty, was soon impressed into carrying urgent cases from the out-stations to the base hospitals at Dogura or Eroro.

The patients might vary from an excommunicate woman suffering from the results of an abortion to the victim of a crocodile attack whose mother darted into the plane and crouched beneath a seat, remaining there throughout the flight. She was really a plucky woman, for Papuan women did not take readily to modern

H

medical aids. When Dr Blanche Biggs in her tuberculosis hospital was rejoicing over the arrival of her X-ray plant, a deputation of uneasy patients approached her and said, "Please would you take our picture and then we can go home."

As soon as he returned to Gona, Father Benson put up temporary hospital buildings. For two years he had no trained nurse to replace Sister Hayman, but he had a group of young Papuans who worked under his direction. Sister Nancy Elliott arrived in 1948 and within ten years had made St Raphael's Hospital, Gona, into a notable hospital. The buildings were largely the work of Father John Wardman, who was priest-in-charge in 1951, and though the staff at Gona, as elsewhere, never consciously imitated the methods of Albert Schweitzer, the environment, native custom and hard economics produced many similarities to Lambarene's hospital.

The walls of St Raphael's were made of kipa — wooden sticks strung together and built directly into the sand-dirt floors. The roofs were made of sago palm or corrugated iron. The buildings consisted of an out-patients section, an operating-theatre and labour ward, with other wards as separate buildings. These received a welcome shade from the tulip-trees planted by May Hayman and Mavis Parkinson.

By 1959 there were sixty beds, but the Papuan custom of one or more relatives accompanying the patient to hospital sometimes made the wards overcrowded. The husband came to hospital with his wife, the wife and family with the husband, and both parents with a sick child. Officially one guardian only was supposed to accompany each patient, but after Sister went her rounds at night the relatives, who had been waiting quietly in the shadows, would slip in, light their little fires beneath or by the beds, and tuck the piglets and puppies in with them. There *was* official disapproval whenever it was found that as the chill of the early morning had proved too much for the family, the patient had been lifted from his bed and left to curl up on the floor while the family took his place. The smoky little fires made it difficult at times to see from one end of the ward to the other, but they kept away the mosquitoes that swarmed in from the swamplands. At 6 a.m. the fires would be out, and the wards clean and tidy.

Improvization was the keynote to much work in the operating-theatre. An anaesthetic mask might be simply a cheese tin with the ends cut off, pressed into an oval shape, and with wire gauze over the end. A snake might pass through the theatre during an operation. At night there was always the risk of fire from using highly inflammable anaesthetics near the open flare of a Tilley lamp.

The routine at St Raphael's in 1960 may be taken as typical of the Anglican Mission hospitals in the decade from 1955 to 1965. The Papuan orderlies comprised a medical evangelist, a dispenser-laboratory technician, seven medical boys and six medical girls. The Papuan staff attended lectures and demonstrations and a number would go to St Margaret's, Eroro, to finish their training. Besides administering and preparing mixtures, injections and dressings, and the general care of in-patients and out-patients, the staff took turns in the age-old task of cutting grass, collecting and chopping firewood, washing and ironing the hospital linen, and getting materials from the bush to keep the buildings in good repair. Each week some went on patrol to the villages, giving anti-malarial drugs to all the young children, conducting the baby clinics which saved so many children from death through malnutrition, cerebral malaria and other tropical illnesses. At the baby clinics the weekly doses of Nivaquin were administered to all children under five to prevent them from getting malaria.

Tropical ulcers were until 1959 taking up more of the staff's time than any other disease, and skin grafts to heal the large ones were the commonest operations. Hookworm infestation, filarial infection and other intestinal parasites were common. There was the usual run of coughs, colds, pneumonia, boils. The relationship with the government hospital set up at Saiho, some thirty miles inland, was excellent and it would take patients for X-ray or infants when St Raphael's resources had become overtaxed.

Most of the drugs and equipment were now being supplied by the Department of Health in Port Moresby, though the supply of linen and many useful articles of furniture came through friends. Co-operation was the spirit of government and mission. There was plenty of work for both. The staff at St Raphael's and other hospitals of the mission were greatly cheered by the understanding of the government doctor who, after his inspections, would say, "I do not worry about your buildings. It is the work which goes on inside these buildings that I value."

By 1961 St Raphael's was handling ten thousand out-patient

attendances a month, with a thousand infants coming to the clinics. The hospital radius of sixty miles does not sound far, but a patrol might involve a seven-day journey up the coast and back, with the aid of the *Maclaren King II*, jeep, canoes and bicycles. Sister Colby-Clarke who replaced Sister Elliott when she took over St Luke's tuberculosis and leper hospital in 1959 introduced travel by bicycles. She found there were drawbacks when, to reach a village a few miles away, she encountered eighteen rivers, many of them waist- or even neck-high. Her medical orderly just hoisted both bicycles over his shoulder, crossed the river, came back for her, and lifted her on his shoulders like a sack of kapok.

On a patrol into the Ambasi district Sister Colby-Clarke brought back with her fifty-one patients, the result of an anti-yaws campaign that ultimately eliminated yaws from the district. The enormous tropical ulcers penetrating to the bone were now more rarely seen, and tuberculosis was being brought under control. Cerebral malaria and whooping cough, which took the lives of so many babies, were defeated by immunization. Anaemia, the cause of which was still uncertain, remained the great problem.

In 1960 the Anglican Mission had a total of 3 training hospitals, 6 hospitals with trained sisters in charge, 11 with trained medical evangelists in charge, and 12 dispensaries in the charge of teacher-evangelists. The base hospital for the southern archdeaconry was St Barnabas's, Dogura, and in the northern archdeaconry, St Margaret's, Eroro. The base hospitals are training hospitals and drug supply depots for the various station hospitals and dispensaries. At the base hospital girls are trained as nurses and boys as hospital assistants. The training is for four years, a comprehensive course with all lectures and instructions in English. The trainees are taught to do minor surgery, such as sutures, incisions, teeth extractions. They must be acquainted with practical obstetrics and infant welfare. They learn to go out on patrol with a Sister or doctor, and then on their own. Some areas are visited fortnightly, others monthly. The sick and undernourished are escorted back to hospital if necessary.

Tuberculosis, introduced by the white man to New Guinea, took hold upon a particularly susceptible population. Forty of the beds at St Margaret's, Eroro, were occupied with tuberculosis cases in 1959 when the government was able to allot money for the building of St Luke's tuberculosis hospital. St Luke's opened with an initial ninety-two beds but with the foundations, drains and sewerage for expansion to a three-hundred-bed hospital. The site of the hospital, Embi, would be known to Australians who fought in the Buna campaign. Throughout the 1960s the government tuberculosis teams have been examining people and bringing in those in need of treatment; some patients have required hospital attention for as long as two years.

At St Barnabas's Hospital, Dogura, there was a surgeon-clergy co-operation rarely found elsewhere in the world. At the operating-table Canon John Chisholm would quietly ask for a blessing on the patient, the surgeon, the anaesthetist and the medical attendants. The congregation of Dogura Cathedral would pray daily for the sick by name, and attend the burial service of those who died far from their villages and friends. The ordered peace and efficiency of Dogura were appreciated by a government even more short of trained staff than the missions.

In New Britain where the Anglican Mission was acutely conscious of its deficiencies, in the highlands both of Papua and the Trust Territory of New Guinea, the trained medical evangelists were pioneers bringing healing of mind and body to those who previously could turn only to the sorcerer. Each out-station has its small school, and first aid is rendered by the teacher to the children of the village. The Administration and the mission hospitals seldom have overlapping areas, and the Administration supplies the drugs and essentials. Patrols are arranged by agreement, and mission medical officers are given the opportunity to accompany assistant district officers on their patrols.

At Movi, the hospital in the remote western highlands of New Guinea, Sister Bridget Irwin with her partially trained Papuan nurses had five wards, each with about twenty patients (plus relatives), a hundred out-patients a day. Twice a day she became a radio operator to consult a doctor about urgent cases. The establishment of a radio network (1964) through the Christian Radio Missionary Fellowship meant that many stations, boats and aeroplanes could join; this service was invaluable in emergencies. The *St Gabriel* could be called upon to bring to hospital a patient whose chance of life depended upon immediate treatment.

Camoquin tablets were now used to ward off the great killer, malaria. In the highlands there were still cases of elephantiasis, causing swelling of limbs, and ulcers that could rot right through a leg. The childbirth mortality rate was twenty-five times that of Australia; the chief causes were anaemia, lack of antenatal supervision, and lack of attention during difficult labours. Too often the mission station is called upon too late to save the mother or child. The people of the highlands accept pain with remarkable tolerance and are reluctant to bring the sick to hospital if it means a journey of several days. The children accept tooth-pulling without anaesthetic or fuss. Men and women breathe in their anaesthetic as calmly as they would smoke a cigarette or chew a betelnut. After operations there is no request for pain-killers. High blood-pressure and duodenal ulcers are unknown, and there is a rarity of heart disease, possibly because of a low-fat diet and lifelong physical activity. Cancer seems to be restricted to the mouth, probably as a result of chewing betel-nut and quick-lime.

In the Papuan highlands Dr Charles Elliott found one case of schizophrenia, a village boy who spoke good English and had experienced considerable contact with Europeans. In his weird schizophrenic moods he became Slim Dusty, a cowboy of the Wild West. "Two of them have left and I am going too, out of this place," he would shout, as he waved his imaginary six-shooter. He was in a constant state of terror.

In 1964, at the request of the Public Health Department, the mission station at Simbai, under the charge of Papuan medical orderly, Byron Sevesi, and with Sister Olive Robin supervising, took over sole responsibility for an area of three hundred square miles, with a population of twelve thousand. His staff consisted of six Papuan medical orderlies. There were two bush hospitals, four out-station aid posts, and three infant welfare centres with an enrolment of four hundred mothers and their babies.

At Koinambe the patient work, involved in antenatal advice and infant welfare, anti-malarial treatments and immunizations against whooping cough, brought in 1967 a new worry to Sister Olive Robin, wife of the priest-in-charge. She was struck by an excessive number of subnormal children all under the age of five. She reported to Dr Ian Butterfield, a research fellow in medicine from Adelaide University, who investigated and found that 18 per cent of the people were mentally subnormal, but that all were children under five. A research team from Adelaide University and the Public Health Department is giving iodized oil injections to pregnant mothers. It is the first time doctors have had an opportunity to establish the iodine deficiency link by controlled experiment. In the customary tribal life, most of the children would have died and the few subnormals who survived would have been absorbed by the tribe. Sister Olive and Canon Robin face the problem of the special education needed for the children whose lives have been saved.

By 1967 the people of the highlands were showing increasing confidence in seeking mission help in their illnesses. The registers at the stations showed over a thousand treatments a month, and at one centre there was an attendance of three thousand in one month.

In the Managalas highlands of Papua Sister Nancy Vesperman waited through 1966 and 1967, at the primitive hospital her Papuan staff had built, for village women to decide to come to her for assistance in childbirth. She was met one day by a group of village men carrying a groaning, struggling woman to the hospital. They had seen the woman was having great trouble in labour, and one man had suggested taking her to the hospital. An hour before the baby was born she staggered off into the bush and had to be brought back again. The successful birth and the news that "Mother and child were doing well" spread through the village, and there was a rush of visitors — some to stay. When Sister Vesperman went off again on her hygiene patrols, equipped with posters, she realized that from now on there would be a different attitude towards her lonely and primitive hospital.

Down on the coast the experienced Dr Blanche Biggs was feeling that her years of organizing medical work with two pairs of forceps and a roll of cotton wool had gone on for far too long. The old mission policy, enforced as it was, of putting up bush buildings was now neither cheap nor useful. Cartage was becoming more expensive than the materials merited. The buildings were inadequate and always likely to sag sideways or fall down. The efficiency of a sister-in-charge who was expert alike in teaching, hygiene, patrol work, surgery, obstetrics, child welfare, as well as building repair, book-keeping, gardening and jungle control, was suspect in some Public Health Department quarters. But the Government, which might produce funds for special hospitals, such as the tuberculosis hospitals, which the mission would staff, was chary about providing funds for hospitals that would be on mission lands. There had to be an application of "Self-help for the Papuans" policy with what funds could be secured from Australia.

St Margaret's Hospital, Eroro, was on an undrainable site. It was decided to transfer it to nearby Katereda, where there was a ridge forty feet high with a magnificent view of Oro Bay and a creek that would give an abundant water supply. The people of Eroro and of neighbouring villages sent teams of workers; with picks, shovels, a wheelbarrow, plus improvised trays, they succeeded in getting the site level within two months. From villages farther out teams came to work for a week at a time, digging out huge basalt boulders which they broke into pieces of manageable size by building fires around them until they cracked. The new St Margaret's Hospital was finished by the beginning of 1968, to the delight of the doctor, Maurice Dowell, and his wife, Mary, the nurse, who had worked at Eroro for twelve years, and who, after furlough and study in England and America, have returned to St Margaret's at Oro Bay.

The entire cost of the hospital was met by the Australian Church, much of it raised personally by Mrs Gladys Dahlenberg of Melbourne. The hospital was built by the mission's building team, the Oro Bay Builders. A modern building of six wards, with eighty beds, a well-equipped operating-theatre, electricity and a good water supply, the entire cost — in materials and equipment — of erecting the new hospital was $50,000, the price of a fashionable Australian home unit.

12

"...The Beginnings of Wisdom"

THE VITALITY of a school lies not in functional buildings but in the comradeship of endeavour that welds together pupils, staff, parents and ex-pupils. When the buildings of the Martyrs School were destroyed, the school was immediately re-established at Gona with the remnant of its pupils. Then the villagers of Agenehambo offered a large area of land in the jungle on which new buildings might be erected. The pupils who had survived the eruption cleared the land, with alternate shifts working or in the classroom. A school was built with materials cut from the surrounding bush. The classrooms were large and adequate; the chapel became a source of pride to the boys.

Edward Marriott, an airline pilot and University graduate, offered his services to the Bishop as acting headmaster. Later he came to Brisbane and talked with the Reverend Byam Roberts, headmaster of the Slade School, which under his charge had established a brilliant scholastic reputation. It seemed to Byam Roberts that his duty lay in Papua, and it was agreed that he should offer himself as priest-headmaster of the Martyrs School. Father Roberts, Edward Marriott ("Brother" Ted) and Brother Bevan Meredith (now Bishop) were the pioneer teachers who set the high standards of the Martyrs School and won for it the good name and high prestige it holds today.

By 1955 the standard attained in the academic subjects taught, including English, history, geography and mathematics, was approximately equal to the New South Wales Intermediate Cer-

tificate — that is, three years' secondary education.* In all schools
of the Anglican Mission, English was used from Standard III
upwards, but at Martyrs the language throughout the school was
English. By 1960 the principal was assisted by three Australian
trained teachers and a staff of specially picked and competent
Papuans.

In the early years of the school, the boys had reached an
Australian educational level of 10-plus when they sat for the
admission examination. The school day consisted of teaching from
8.30 a.m. to 3.30 p.m., then outside work and games. Evensong
was at 5.30 p.m. followed by dinner, three-quarters of an hour
free time, then lesson preparation. The boys were trained in self-
support, growing their own food and learning to be independent.
The diocese allowed £1,000 a year to cover all salaries and
expenses. The government gave nothing, and there were 180
boys to feed. It was part of the school's training that every boy
should produce an average of 35 pounds' weight of vegetables
each week. The vegetables were weighed into the school store and
then issued and cooked for meals. There was and could be no
outside assistance to the school. Every one of the jobs required
to keep it going had to be shared by teachers and pupils. There
had to be a constant watch on the weather and against insects of
every kind. The bush had to be kept back, the grass cut, timber
felled and pitsawn, buildings kept in repair, the dispensary staffed.

It was Geelong Grammar School which gave the greatest moral
and financial support to Martyrs Memorial School. In 1964 the
senior history master wrote. "We here at Geelong Grammar are
very conscious of Martyrs, for we have come over the past four
years to regard it as our brother school." The help began in a
modest way — the gift of a tractor, a trailer and saw-bench. Then
in 1961, when Dr (Sir) James Darling was retiring from the
headmastership of Geelong Grammar, he requested that money
collected as a present to him should be given to Martyrs. With the
help of a fair, some £3,000 was raised for new buildings and
greatly needed electrical equipment. By 1964 the traditional

*cf. R. S. Parker, in *New Guinea on the Threshold*, Ed. E. K. Fisk (A.N.U.
Press, Canberra), p. 245: "At the beginning of the 1950s there were about
100,000 indigenous children receiving primary education, and these almost
entirely in mission schools and attaining a rudimentary level of bare literacy;
there was not one indigene receiving secondary or tertiary education of any
kind."

buildings, which represented so much endeavour, so much self-respect and educational training, had largely given way to European buildings, including a laboratory and library and a two-storey mission house. There were new teachers' quarters and a new dispensary.

Geelong Grammar School boys pay annual visits to Martyrs, and three boys from Martyrs stayed at Geelong in one visit. Funds were raised to permit a Papuan boy to attend Geelong Grammar in 1966. When the party from Geelong visited Martyrs in that year, it included Prince Charles. At Dogura Cathedral there was a congregation of two thousand of whom nine hundred took Holy Communion with the Prince. He visited the Franciscan Friary at Jegarata, St Christopher's Manual Training School, and then travelled along the sixteen-mile bumpy track to Martyrs. Here the traditional welcome of an ambush of befeathered, spear-brandishing warriors was given him. The party stayed five days, playing games, swimming, hiking. When the Prince left, the people of Agenehambo, after an afternoon of dancing, feasting and games, presented him with the Otohu necklace, the symbol of a chieftain, from the Orokaiva tribe.

The 1969 postings of the Australian Board of Missions show the Venerable Byam Roberts, for years headmaster of Martyrs Memorial Secondary School, now Diocesan Director of Education, living in Port Moresby.

The sister school to Martyrs is the Holy Name School founded by the Sisters of the Holy Name at Dogura in 1955. Here, biology, domestic science and sewing are counterparts to the boys' physics, agriculture and handicrafts. The establishment of a secondary school for girls was a new and important departure, for while most Papuan villagers are anxious that their boys should be educated, they regard the departure of their girls to boarding-school with suspicion. For this reason the Holy Name School in its early years took girls only from nearby villages. With the spread of education in New Guinea, much of the prejudice has died, and an important feature of the school is its preparation of girls to go on to train as teachers.

St Paul's School, Dogura, is the senior school of the Anglican Mission. Its traditions date back to the arrival and teachings of Bishop Stone-Wigg and Henry Newton. As a boarding-school its numbers fluctuate with the changing fortunes of the mission station schools. When these have been satisfactorily staffed, the boarders decline at St Paul's. With the spread of education in the highlands, the boarders increased, the latest figures showing some fifty boarders from the highlands sent to St Paul's to the higher standards. Some one hundred and fifty come from out-stations, walking for distances up to six hours' adult walking; they arrive on a Monday morning and return on the Friday.

The government school inspectors are men of integrity grounded in the principles of nineteenth-century Manchester colonialism. When they inspected St Paul's in 1962, they reported favourably on the academic standards but requested that the boys should give up their traditional aras and wear shorts and that the girls should no longer wear the native skirts but dresses. The gentle Sisters of the Holy Name had never hesitated to be photographed in their white habits standing with their girls. The boys, whose sonorous singing in Dogura Cathedral was a source of wonderment to visitors and who, clad only in their aras, moved with such dignity as servers at the consecration and enthronement of bishops, were perplexed. The staff was more so. The cost of a minimum of two pairs of shorts per boy each year and two dresses per girl would take one-third of what the school received each year in assistance from the government.

An example of the pioneer women Papuan teachers would be Ivy Awui, daughter of a Papuan priest, who completed the full Registration Course for teachers and then, with one assistant, set to teaching sixty-eight children in Standard III at Holy Cross School, Gona. But a more typical present-day example of the effect of mission education would be the case of Grace Maude, a bright girl who came dux of the school at Gona, then returned happily and voluntarily as a pupil teacher for three years. Then she married and came to St Raphael's Maternity Hospital for the difficult birth of her second child. As her children grew older, she became a vice-president of the Women's Club and one of the instigators in the building of a clubroom and clinic-room. Her Women's Club runs a village laundry and, when the young men return from Port Moresby in their smart shorts and shirts, they can have these washed and ironed professionally by the club — the proceeds going to the club funds. The club has regular village meetings for songs and games, and its leaders inspect the houses of nearby villages giving prizes for the neatest and best.*

There were after the war few Papuans skilled in building or carpentry. At the growing Administrative centre of Popondetta, Rodd Hart set up St Christopher's Manual Training School. A mechanic himself, he was for years the school's sole instructor. The first buildings were the usual native-style sheds, but in them carpentry was taught. By 1958 the principal was able to report on the building of a new school house, Sangara House, a European-type timber frame building with an iron roof. The walls were of scrap that was collected from a local sawmill and sawn into useful sizes on the school mill. Roughly six thousand lineal feet of timber was all *hand-planed* by the students, as well as a couple of sanded panels inside the building. The cost of Sangara House to the Anglican Mission was £80.

The creek between the Church and Primary School of the Resurrection, Popondetta, and St Christopher's is spanned by a truck chassis rescued and shaped into a bridge by the boys. The concrete floor slab and one wall of the coffee house in which May Hayman and Mavis Parkinson were imprisoned still remain on the original site fifty feet from this bridge. By 1965, from bits and pieces of the war of twenty years before, the school had assembled twelve jeeps. These formed the mission fleet for miles around, and their maintenance was carried out by the school. The pupils took great pride in the perfect condition of a former United States Army 10-wheeler G.M. transport.

By 1965 the school subjects included all normal academic subjects, as well as technical drawing, mechanical drawing, woodwork and mechanical engineering. A joinery class involved students in the most delicate wood-carving. On Sundays the boys formed the choir at the Church of the Resurrection.

The pattern of primary education in the Anglican Mission had been established long before the middle of this century. There were two types of primary schools, the little village school and the

*cf. Sir A. Grenfell Price's story of the Papuan librarian trained for several years by the government. "My bride-price," she said, "is now about £1,000. A tribe will buy me for some young man. He will never allow me to go back to librarianship, and I will spend the rest of my life looking after him and our children." *The Challenge of New Guinea* (Angus and Robertson, Sydney), p. 129.

central school where the mission had its local station. The village
school might have only one teacher, and the language was normally the local language up to Standard II. Many of the village
schools did not go beyond that standard. At the mission station
there was either a European teacher in charge or a more highly
qualified and experienced Papuan teacher, with assistants. Children came in to the mission station to board when they attained
a required standard.

An example of a mission station school in 1953 would be that
at Agenehambo, where Mrs Betty Porter was assisted by fifteen
Papuan teachers to teach six hundred pupils. At Sasembata and at
Gona there were schools of three hundred pupils each. At Wani-
gela the lower grades were taught in three different languages.
At Eroro there were no less than eighteen out-station schools.

The educational principle of the Anglican Mission was firmly
laid down: *English is the only solution to the language problem
in Papua*. Within the area of the mission there were six entirely
different languages, to say nothing of the innumerable dialects.
"English is the only possible solution to the unity of New Guinea,"
affirmed the Australian Board of Missions, "and unity there must
be as the people grow into a nation."* This was in 1956.

It was, however, the conviction of the mission educationists
that the teaching of English could be best achieved only when
the student thoroughly understood and could read and write in
his own language. There was some concern when a high official
in the Administration attempted to set a policy that English should
be taught from the earliest grades in all schools. This would have
been disastrous, when it is considered how few Papuan teachers
were capable of teaching English really adequately. In an address
to a conference of New Guinea missionary representatives in 1956
Paul Hasluck made it clear that the government did not intend to
lay down policy how English teaching was to be attained.

In one important respect the Church differed from the
Administration in those years when the government was feeling
its way, as it still is, towards an educational policy. It would be
a fair thing to say the majority of those officers of the Administra-

*cf. O. H. K. Spate in *New Guinea on the Threshold*, ed. E. K. Fisk
(A.N.U. Press, Canberra), p. 119. "In one important respect some mission
education has had rather a negative effect; this is the preference for teaching
in Pidgin or in indigenous languages."

tion who had any basic educational philosophy in the 1950s held to a vague nineteenth-century liberalism. The policy of the Anglican Church was clearly defined: *"Education without any philosophy of life ceases to be education;* it is simply a jumble of facts that tend to confuse rather than to unify all, save perhaps the very best minds."

The Church sought in her schools to introduce the child to her Lord. Her teachers were required to be men of character as well as firmly grounded in the Christian religion and speaking good English. To send a man whose academic attainments were satisfactory, but who did not come up to expectations in other respects, to a lonely position of responsibility without supervision was a risk that could not be taken. More than one reject from the Anglican Mission was taken up with alacrity by the Education Department.

Since 1917 St Aidan's College, which was established then by Henry Newton, has been training teacher-evangelists. After the Second World War the teachers sent out by St Aidan's did much in the war-stricken areas to stabilize and restore village life where the people had been deprived of their leaders. From 1941 to 1960 it was under the charge of Oliver John Brady, a Master of Arts of Melbourne University and a graduate in theology. By 1961 when the government's educational policy was more clearly defined, it was the aim of St Aidan's that all its men should secure the Education Department's certificate of registration, either at the lower A or the higher B certificate. In 1959, of the forty-seven candidates presented by St Aidan's for the Administration's Teacher Certificate examinations, forty-five passed and its students topped the list in both the Certificate A and B examinations. It was a record not equalled by any other authority in the territory. The men could choose to enter the teaching service of the government or of the Anglican Mission. Almost all chose to become mission teachers. By 1967 there were over four hundred St Aidan's four-year-trained men serving in the mission schools.

In 1961 the Bishop of New Guinea established St Hilda's Teaching Training College for Papuan girls at Dogura, but a few years later the government announced a policy of co-educational training for all teachers. St Hilda's became a hostel for the girls, who from then on had their training at St Aidan's.

It may be of interest to critics of mission schools in New Guinea to quote here some figures relative to their treatment by the Australian government in past years. In 1939 there were no government schools whatever in Papua, and the 416 mission (station) schools received between them a grant of £3,101. In the Mandated Territory of New Guinea £8,274 was spent on six government schools, and the 2,566 mission schools received nothing. Between 1948–49 and 1958–59 mission schools in Papua–New Guinea rose to 4,205 with 171,453 pupils, 685 non-native teachers, and 5,782 native teachers. At this time the grant to the Diocese of New Guinea rose to a little less than 10s. per annum per pupil.

In 1964 the International Bank Report pointed out: "It is most important that the co-operation of the missions in the education of the indigenes should be continued and extended. . . . The subsidy to mission primary schools amounted to £A340,000 in 1962–63 or approximately £A3 per pupil in registered and recognized schools (as compared with a cost per pupil of £A30 in Administration primary schools). In the future this figure appears likely to be insufficient."

By 1965, after thirteen years of intensive educational drive by the government, there were 66,888 pupils in the 492 schools of the Administration, compared with 189,381 children in the 3,639 mission schools. Out of an expenditure of £3,960,000 on education, the grants-in-aid to mission schools were £489,000, while the missions were spending £907,000 from their own funds. To correct the apparent conclusion that the government was allotting one-eighth of its education grant to the schooling of three-quarters of New Guinea's pupils, it needs to be remembered that the government by now was paying an indirect sum in school supplies, allowances for teacher trainees and travel allowances. The charge that the mission schools were not providing education of a satisfactory standard is met by the fact that the number of indigenous children in mission schools registered as satisfactory by government inspectors rose from 70,237 in 1960 to 129,560 in 1965.

The Report of an Ecumenical Visit to New Guinea in June 1965 pointed out:

It should be clear that churches and missions cannot accept a view of education which is concerned only with educational standards and

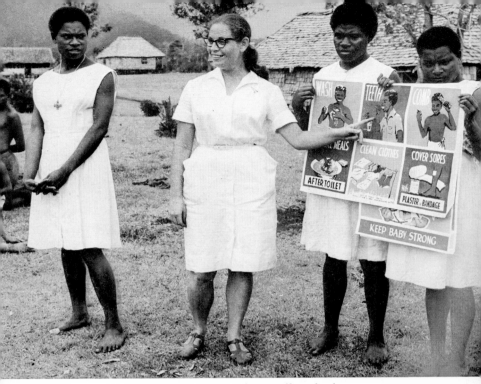

*Sister Nancy Vesperman gives a talk on hygiene
to villagers at Sakarina in Papua.*

Lay evangelists talk to villagers in the Managalas district of Papua.

Villagers in the Managalas district waiting to be baptized
at the first baptism to be held in the area — November 1966.

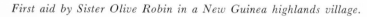

First aid by Sister Olive Robin in a New Guinea highlands village.

the production of an élite. Nor can they accept the view implicit in the International Bank Report that education is for economic development only. While accepting the importance of both of these aims, the churches and missions must, and do, see the fundamental aim to be the well-being and development of the communities and persons of the territory. In short, the development of an élite and of economic resources are not ends but means to improved social life and living which, however it is defined, is the end of education — simply that men and women may have fuller life both as individuals and in the community.*

The representatives of the seven missionary bodies in the Australian Council of Churches then concluded: "Consequently, there is a place for exempt schools and there is a case for reviewing the syllabus of recognized primary schools."†

A well-known Australian educationist tells the story of a visitor to New Guinea who was being shown over one of the expensive government schools. Seeing some white teachers busy in the garden during the luncheon recess, he asked of a couple of students, "Do you boys work in the garden too?" "We come here for white man's learning" was the reply. "If white teachers want garden, they can look after it themselves."

The story, apocryphal or not, illustrates the issue that confronted the Anglican Mission for the early years of this decade. The Report of the Commission on Higher Education in New Guinea (1964) pointed out that, to meet teacher requirements for the target set for 1975, at least 25 per cent of the secondary school children in the territories would need to be recruited as teachers.

The government expenditure on buildings, its "crash" programme of teacher training,‡ its posters advertising "Be a Teacher — Good Pay — Good Holidays — Interesting Work — Good

---

Responsibility in New Guinea, p. 20, Clause 4.23.

†The 1,650 "exempt" mission schools with 55,000 pupils in 1965 are those not reaching the standards required by the government. The majority of these would be in the most backward regions, which are not and cannot be staffed by the Administration; and it might be argued, though the Ecumenical Committee does not do so, that these "exempt" schools are the most in need of assistance.

‡See A. Grenfell Price, *The Challenge of New Guinea* (Angus and Robertson, Sydney), p. 125. A "crash" programme meant taking children to intermediate standard, giving them twelve months' training and sending them out to teach in the schools. The Currie Committee criticized this as a "desperation" course. The Director replied that the position called for desperate measures.

1

Prospects of Promotion", all this put the Church on the defensive. It was natural that a school should be judged by its appearance, the remuneration given its teachers, rather than by its tone, character building and scholastic results. "The Church is lagging behind" was one cry. "Should we not be educating our pupils to enter the government schools to spread the Christian religion there?" was another.

It was the policy of the Anglican Mission to educate the people in their own environment and into that environment. It was the policy of the government to educate an élite out of that environment. In the outer districts the mission was on firm ground. If it had attempted to put up modern buildings, assuming the money was available, what chance would there have been of enticing the superstitious to send their children to them? At the larger schools, away from the towns, the policy of erecting, maintaining and provisioning a school by the combined efforts of staff, parents and pupils was in keeping with the traditions of the great European educators, Froebel and Montessori. In the larger centres the Church was on the defensive.

In June 1964 David Hand, Bishop of New Guinea, was stung into replying to the criticisms of the schools of the diocese. We have, he maintained, many schools that are every bit as good and better than their opposite-number state schools. He quoted the Education Department official who said, "Your Martyrs School boys have it all over ours for character, initiative and self-reliance." (On the staff of Martyrs School at this time there were five university graduates, three matriculated European assistants, and one Papuan c course graduate.) The Bishop pointed out that Papuan parents at one Administration centre were transferring their children from the state school to the mission school because they said the latter was "better". It was easy for officials to criticize school buildings of the missions, without offering any funds for their replacement.*

The Bishop quoted the New Guinea Director of Education, who, in answering the question, "What makes a good school?" replied, "I have no hesitation in claiming that the first and most important job of the school is to produce proud students." It was a "starry-eyed" concept, said the Bishop, to imagine that the

---

*See photographs in E. K. Fisk (ed.), *New Guinea on the Threshold* (A.N.U. Press, Canberra), p. 29.

Church could "drench every corner of the state educational sphere with the Church's gospel". It was the Anglican Mission's policy to make the Church school system as extensive and influential as availability of money and staff would allow. The Church was not in "bleak" opposition to the government school system; she attempted to be a greatly needed leavening complement. She was, however, in opposition in the sense that she upheld an entirely different philosophy of education and purpose from the Government's.

The probable attitude of a self-governing New Guinea to mission schools was expressed by John Guise when he was elected leader of the elected members of the House of Representatives in Papua–New Guinea. "Every member of the present Legislative Council of Papua–New Guinea," he pointed out, "every member both elected and appointed is an ex-Church school boy, including myself. When we have our national government I am sure that no national government in Papua–New Guinea would interfere with Church schools simply because we owe our very existence today to Church schools." John Guise described himself as a product of the Anglican Church.

13

In the Highlands

ON THE Feast of the Precious Blood, 11th July 1959, Father Peter Robin celebrated the Holy Communion at an improvised altar on Togban Ridge in the western highlands of New Guinea. There was a special significance to the service, for two years before on the Ridge had occurred the last of the inter-tribal skirmishes of the highland people. The Togbanites, for sheer mischief, had raided the Kwiop people, killing twenty-two of them, chiefly women and children. The government officer from Mount Hagen had come north with armed police, but was repulsed and had to retire for reinforcements. Then followed the skirmish on Togban Ridge when the Togbanites lost four of their men killed and were compelled to make a "pay-back" of girls to marry into the Kwiop. Atop the ridge now stood a giant rough timber cross flanked by the Anglican Mission station and a government rest-house.

The presence of the Church in one of the wildest regions of New Guinea was a result of six years' planning under the leadership of David Hand. He then had charge of the Northern Archdeaconry, which included New Britain and the Trust Territory of New Guinea. When the eastern highlands of the territory had been partly explored during the gold strikes of the 1930s, Roman Catholic and Lutheran missionaries had moved in, turning south from Lae. The Anglican Diocese of New Guinea, which was in reality a diocese of north Papua, had been in no position to undertake a new area.

By 1953 there was a road running through the alluvial valley from Lae through Goroka and on to Mount Hagen; but air travel was the chief means of transport. Of the 2,000,000 people of Papua–New Guinea, some 750,000 live in the highlands, where everything from bananas to lettuces will grow. There live the stone-age men with their gaudy decorations of shells and plumes, their wigs of human hair, their skilfully made axes and clubs of stone.

The area in which Bishop Hand asked for permission to operate was a "restricted area": that is to say, no one was allowed to enter it without official approval. The Administration was, under the Freedom of Religion clause of the United Nations Charter, permitting sects of every conceivable nature, well-backed by American dollars, into all other parts of the territory, but delayed for three years a satisfactory reply to the Assistant Bishop's plea for access to people cut off from every form of medical and educational help. The region where the Roman Catholic Church and the Lutherans were working was well to the east and south.

The Anglican Church wished to work in the district between the Ramu and Jimi rivers. Reference to a map will show a series of parallel geographical features. There is the northern coast on which lies Madang, once the administrative capital of German New Guinea and now the fourth largest town in the territory. Parallel to the coast, and cutting off Madang from the interior, is the Adelbert Range. Then in another parallel line, farther south, is the valley of the Ramu River. South of this the Schrader and Bismarck ranges form another parellel line. Then there is the valley of the Jimi River. The Ramu flows north-west into the sea, and the Jimi into the great Sepik River.

Half-way along the course of the Ramu River, on the south side, there was an airstrip and patrol post. Some twenty minutes' walk away was the first village of mountain people — pygmies. The Assistant Bishop decided to set up a "doorway" mission station at Aiome while waiting for the government to make up its mind about giving leave to go beyond.

Then came an offer of land in the Siane district, in another part of the highlands south-east of Goroka, from a sympathetic planter, and this permitted David Hand in 1955 to take in some Papuan teacher-evangelists with the aid of the *St Gabriel*. The Siane people proved friendly, and in Holy Week of 1956 Bishop Hand took in the first group of Melanesian Brothers in response to the request of the highland people for more missionaries.

The Brothers set up a mission station at Movi, where Dr June Stephenson and Sister Blake established St Saviour's Hospital. Then the Brothers moved on to Lende at the head of the valley and almost at the boundary of the Siane and Chuave districts. There on a beautiful site, which had the advantages of water and good garden land, they built a magnificent church, the Church of the Holy Cross.

Meanwhile a permit had come for the Anglican Mission to enter the Schrader mountain area, into the Asai and Simbai valleys, a most rugged terrain in which a scattered and semi-nomadic population of pygmies lives. They have no villages; three or four houses make up a hamlet. They were riddled with fear and superstition. Vendettas were part of their daily life, but the manner of killing was furtive and mean. They did not bury their dead, but left them to rot and then kept the bones in the house. Men would melt into the bush when they saw a missionary approaching. Girls were kept hidden from the time of weaning until they were of a marriageable age. The terrain was desperately rugged, formed or cleared walking tracks being almost non-existent, except in the Jimi valley.

At the head of the Simbai River was a small strip of land where the *St Gabriel* might land. There the mission station of St Laurence was set up, later to be joined by a Government patrol post. A lay missionary, Tom Watson, pioneered bush stations through the Asai and Simbai valleys, setting up the little bush schools, neat, compact and solid buildings. This was the work of three years of arduous patrols in which the Assistant Bishop played a large part. Five years later a boy was sent from Aiome mission station to the Martyrs School to be trained as a teacher to his own people.

By 1961 the Anglican Mission had some forty missionaries working in the Schraders — Melanesian Brothers and Papuan teachers, some of these with their wives. Among the friendly Siane people great progress had been made in five years. There were six schools supervised by Mrs Dawn Kenyon, recognized by the Department of Education, and staffed by Papuan teachers trained at St Aidan's and with registration certificates. There were six hundred school children and some three thousand five hundred catechumens. Forty of the more promising boys had been sent to the boarding-school of St Paul's, Dogura. One Siane man had been given a provisional licence as a medical worker.

In Holy Week 1961, after years of instruction and example from the Papuan staff, Franklin Otoha and his wife Dulcie were able to present 536 catechumens for baptism. The serious business of sorting, testing and selecting the candidates, the hearing of four to five hundred confessions, occupied Bishop Hand and his clergy for the whole of three days. The candidates had brought with them gifts, vegetables, mats and trade tobacco, soap, four pigs and twenty-eight chickens. In the interviews there had to be keen examination of those whose records were unsatisfactory and others who merely wished "not to be left off the bandwagon".

On Good Friday, following the custom of the diocese which enjoins silence as well as fasting until the late afternoon, a Via Dolorosa service was held. Stations of the Cross were observed at small casuarina crosses which had been erected the day before. Here short addresses were given and simple repetitive prayers. The scene on Easter Eve is described by David Hand:

By noon on Easter Eve, all were arranged in serried ranks on the slopes beyond the stream. Many Christians from Nambaiyufa (baptized last November) joined as sponsors, with the Papuan and European staff and Anglican visitors from the nearest government station. On the station-side slopes, literally thousands of onlookers (and silent participants) gathered from many miles around. The making of the Promises and the Recital of the Creed were booms of thunder, and then the great host of candidates began slowly enfilading down to the stream, each accompanied by his or her sponsor; through the threefold washing; up, born again, to change in the schoolroom into their baptismal white garments. At the door of the church they received their lighted candles and made their offerings. First in the line was their acknowledged leader, disciple of the Brothers and interpreter for every instruction for five years — the luluai [government-acknowledged natural chief man]. He speaks in a voice which would make a fog-horn green with envy. His native name, as the people say it, is almost YAHWEH. He has been a great visitor of wrath on the children of disobedience, be they young or old. We thought we could almost visualize him going up to those big white rocky cliffs on the mountainside above Lende and coming back with the Ten Commandments inscribed on one of them and smashing it to smithereens over Fikombaro! So we could but call him Moses; for also he had led his people through the wilderness of heathendom. . . .*

In the morning, as the sun broke through the mist (late as always in these mountains) the crowds were winding along the tracks to take part in their first full eucharist and to hear again the thrilling story of the Empty Tomb. Father Dams "conducted" the eucharist from well-prepared notes in the Siane language, as we have not yet managed to get the liturgy translated. The service drew to its climax; the silence could almost be felt; and again, as the tiny bell tinkled happily in the sanctuary, "came Jesus and stood in the midst", and we — His 536 new disciples — "were glad when we saw the Lord".

In the Schraders, in the valleys of Asai and Simbai, the eucharists offered by Canon Peter Robin were lonely ones for years. At Koinambe Sister Olive Robin set up her baby clinic and made her discovery of the large number of subnormal children. The government was willing to provide her with medical stores, but equipment was purchased with a special grant of $1,200 given by the Australian Board of Missions.

There were fourteen thousand people in the Simbai valley alone, mostly living a nomadic life in the bush and hard to contact. They were frightened of sorcery and witchcraft, and they had their traditional tribal enemies and outbreaks of fighting between individuals. In 1965 the Reverend John Cottier, who was taking over while Canon Robin pressed on into the Jimi River valley, described them as having pierced noses, large mud wigs, carrying bows and arrows everywhere, and wearing no clothing except a loin cloth. Yet Simbai station was 5,500 feet high with high mountains in all directions, and on clear mornings a beautiful view of Mt Wilhelm, New Guinea's highest mountain, 15,000 feet high. Each afternoon at Simbai there was rain and it became quite cold.

There were as yet no Christians and only a few catechumens. Mrs Judy Cottier persuaded some forty young people to come to school and took the first class herself. None of the people could speak any English and only a very few had a smattering of Pidgin. The missionaries set out on patrols, walking — there was no other way — over the rugged terrain to nearby villages.

In 1967 the Simbai mission station was typical of those now being established in the highlands. It consisted of the priest-in-charge, his wife — in this case a teacher, though often it would be

*Moses Yauwe now represents his own electoral district in the House of Assembly.

a nursing sister — a certificated Sister, two young volunteers doing voluntary service, one from New Zealand and one from the United Kingdom Volunteers Service Overseas, a nurse and the Papuan teacher-evangelists teaching in the out-stations.

Christmas Day 1967 marked the birth of a Church in this remote part of New Guinea. An Assistant Bishop, the Right Reverend Bevan Meredith, walked for six hours across the Bismarck Range along a jungle track to baptize sixty candidates by total immersion in the nearby river. After baptism the people returned in procession to the bush church, where they were confirmed.

Then the Bishop went on to the Jimi River where a hundred and seventy new Christians were admitted at the out-stations of Kwema and Kompiai, and at Kompiai the ceremonies were followed by a huge sing-sing with five hundred people taking part. In these services in the Jimi River valley the Bishop was assisted by Canon Peter Robin, pioneer of the Church's work in the district, and once the lonely celebrant on Togban Ridge.

14

Towards an Indigenous Church

THE Staff Conferences held at Dogura have marked milestones in the history of the Anglican Mission in New Guinea. In 1947 Bishop Philip Strong delivered his charge, "Out of Great Tribulation", to a conference which included only twenty of those present in 1941. At the conference that farewelled their Bishop in 1962 there were 135 present, 110 Europeans and 25 Papuans. In the conference called by Bishop David Hand in 1964 the indigenous clergy for the first time outnumbered the Europeans. It was just fifty years since Gerald Sharp ordained the first Papuans. Now there were 22 Papuan priests, 19 deacons and 23 ordinands.

The training of the Papuan clergy was rigorous compared with that of the average theological student. After four to five years spent at St Aidan's the teacher went to one of the main primary schools, or he might be sent immediately to take charge of a village school on an out-station. Here he would teach two or three classes as well as manage the school and supervise the assistant teachers. Since he would probably be the only fully trained teacher he would have to prepare programmes and lessons for each class.

As lay-evangelist and pastor of the village church he would conduct daily worship, preaching at several centres on Sundays as well as holding classes for "hearers" (heathens) and paying visits to the sick and old. During the week he would conduct classes for the catechumens or those preparing for confirmation. He would be in demand by the villagers to judge disputes or give advice. He would minister to the dying, bury the dead, comfort and instruct the bereaved.

In his school, registered and inspected by the Government, he was hampered by lack of equipment, shortage of exercise books and textbooks, which the government, because of restricted funds, never adequately supplied. Because the mission is always short of money there was a lack of furniture, pictures, books and modern aids in his school, and he had to fall back on his training to devise local resources for the teaching of art and handicrafts.

From the best of the teacher-evangelists come the men who return to Newton College for further training before being admitted to the diaconate. The tragedy of Mount Lamington set back the creation of a strong indigenous clergy by over a decade. The creation of a permanent diaconate would have laid the Church open to the suspicion that she considered the Papuan was suitable only for an inferior status, that he could be made to serve the white clergy as the "boss-boy" did the trader. But this did not bar the ordination of men who had served a long period in positions of responsibility. In 1957 Bishop Strong admitted five faithful servants to the diaconate, including Andrew Uware, teacher for thirty years and loyal friend of Henry Holland, Edwy Kaib, evangelist for twenty years, and Laurence Modudula, devoted companion to the Bishop for twenty years. When Andrew Uware was ordained at Agenehambo a congregation of a thousand people gathered as a mark of esteem to the Mamba man who had preached the Gospel to them so eloquently in their Orokaivan language.

Typical of the younger men trained by Oliver Brady was Father George Ambo. He had been at Isivita when Mount Lamington erupted, but his life had been spared and he had gone to Newton College for further training before being admitted as deacon. Then after service with a white priest he had been ordained priest. On St Peter's Day 1960 Bishop Strong felt impelled by the Holy Spirit to call upon this man to be the first Papuan bishop.

The Papuan clergy are not free from weaknesses. There was often a tendency in the early days of a Papuan's ministry for a man to slip back into the easy, comfortable life of the tribal elders. A shrewd observer noted how a Papuan priest, conscious of his newly-won dignity, did not feel it incongruous that he should sit on the mission house veranda and watch the white priest helping with the erection of a classroom. It was Romney Gill's and James Benson's constant prayer that they should be given "brown hearts" so that they might think and feel as Papuans, but even the tolerant James Benson was moved to write a quaint, though practical, letter of exasperation after seeing the state of a church where a lovable and upright Papuan had been in charge for some time without supervision.* But by and large the opinion of the Anglican Mission was supported by experience: "The native priest can bear an influence and preach the Gospel in a way that is never possible to the white missionary."

By 1967 the pattern of theological training was changed. The Warden of Newton College described it as preparation for a "streamed ministry". Seventy men were enrolled at St Aidan's that year. Their training as teachers was to fit them for service in a particular field, some to minister to the people of the bush, some to the people with a higher educational standard living near the well-established mission stations, and some to face the new problems of the urban areas where to the present only white clergy had been stationed. Of the seventy, some would be chosen to return to Newton College for training for the priesthood.

There are only about six real towns in Papua–New Guinea, but the rectors of Port Moresby and Lae are acutely conscious of the problems raised by the drift from village to town in search of the material wealth of a white civilization. The old ties of family and tribe are broken or forgotten. The benefits of European culture — literacy and medicine — do not fully compensate for the break-up of native tradition. Young men, half-educated and with no philosophy of life to take the place of tribal traditions, are unfitted for tribal life and a source of trouble in the towns. They meet with casual employment, interspersed with periods of idleness, and the accompanying vices. There are greater opportunities for drunkenness, gambling and prostitution. "It is modern civilization meeting up with isolation," writes the rector of Lae, ". . . the country boy hitting town. With urban life they are detribalized, permitted to do things that for centuries were forbidden (e.g., divorce) and forbidden to do things which for centuries have been traditional and permissible (e.g., the idea of 'pay-back' or revenge)." In the words of Sir Hubert Murray: "Unless the missionary is there to help him, the native is left like a ship with-

Appendix D. Letter from Father James Benson.

out a rudder and will run a great risk of being wrecked in the sea of alien civilization."

The Anglican Society of St Francis came originally to the towns of New Guinea as it came to the help of the people in the East End of London. The Society was founded after the First World War by Brother Douglas who gave up his position as a chaplain at Oxford to live a life of poverty and to share the life of the unemployed on the roads and in the casual wards. Compassion for the destitute and despairing led him, and when others joined him, and some farm buildings were offered as a centre, the Society of St Francis came into existence. By 1958 it had two houses in the East End of London to minister to the outcast and to the coloured people around the docks. At Cambridge there was one to help undergraduates at a time when they either seek or reject a Gospel. It had a school in Dorset and a second friary in Northumberland.

The Bishop of New Guinea challenged the Society several times to come to New Guinea. "When will you ever be ready to come? And when you are ready will it be worth coming?" The community was summoned together and the challenge was accepted. Father Geoffrey came to Koke, the East End of Port Moresby, where men, separated from their wives and families left in the villages, were confronting — either in poverty or with un- accustomed money — social problems without the security and discipline of their village environment.

The fine new buildings of the Church, School and Friary of St Francis, its dispensary and workshop, stand on a hill over- looking Koke. A Brother with a staff of Papuan teachers is respon- sible for the teaching of children in a co-educational school to Standard VI. Furniture is made in the workshop and manual training classes are held. There are study groups for young men and women attending the technical and teacher-training colleges and the Papuan Medical College. From among these will come Papuan leaders under responsible government. Houses have been built for men who ask to live at the mission.

At Jegarata, near Popondetta, is the Franciscan Chapel of the Evangelists, for the Franciscans believe it is their duty to win young Papuans to the Franciscan way of life. But the people of Jegarata call the chapel "our church". It is in an open field, between the friary and the college, and its style, in the form of a

Sepik spirit house, is an imaginative use of indigenous architecture. The altar is freestanding, and the eucharist is celebrated in the midst of the people. All the timber of the furnishings is from one great cedar-tree; the candlesticks are in the shape of wooden drums, a drum is used for the *sanctus* gong, and Solomon Islands melodies for the musical setting of the eucharist. Around the church are preserved stands of jungle "for the birds". The college extends in a large quadrangle around the church. The buildings are of two storeys with wide verandas. In the evening may be heard the voices of the Papuan Brothers singing chants to a guitar accompaniment played by a Solomon Islands Brother.

The present buildings were not achieved without great effort. When the Franciscans came first to Jegarata they began their mission by going on patrol work in the villages. They then went into the Managalas and the New Guinea highlands. They were requested to hold a series of retreats for the New Guinea clergy, and the diocese next asked them to assist in the training of evangelists. There was no money to build the necessary dormitories, the lecture-rooms, the chapel. Verco Cook of the Dennis Taylor Farm came to their aid but was at first forced to fall back on the old methods of erecting buildings with bush materials.

The Franciscans are governed by their Community Chapter in England but are under obedience to the Bishop of New Guinea. They are not maintained by the diocese, however, and the whole expense of keeping a dozen or so friars in New Guinea is met by the Society. The Franciscans are not allowed to appeal for funds, but the generous support of Friends of the Society of St Francis has enabled them to extend their work, steadily.

On St Laurence's Day 1965 the first Papuan to enter the Order, Brother Philip, was admitted to the diaconate.

The story of the Melanesian Brothers is one of the brightest in the history of the Anglican Church in the South Pacific. The Brotherhood is entirely Melanesian in membership and conception. Tall, strapping men of the Solomons, the Brothers take the three vows of poverty, chastity and obedience, which are renewable each year. There is no idea of life vows, although Brother Andrew, who led the group in New Guinea, had served for twenty years. The Brothers receive no money and go wherever they are sent. The first ten who went to New Guinea volunteered for a period of three years. They are evangelists, though some are also teachers, and they may work only in heathen areas. Their first task is always to learn the language of the local people. They dress in a striking uniform of a white shirt and lava-lava with a wide black cincture and a thin white belt with the copper badge of the Brotherhood.

When they were being shown around Papua before going to the western Highlands, they made a shrewd summing-up of the situation in the towns, and in their talks to young people they pointed out the contrast between a life given to service and one to the ambition of money-making. In their very good English they would tell the boys of the station schools of the contrast between the vow of poverty and the greed of money, the vow of chastity with the practice of promiscuity, and the rule of obedience with the prevalence of licence they saw about them. They were quite frank in their approach. In the Solomons, they explained, some young men leaving school would say that they would please themselves and their own bodies and make lots of money while they were young. Then, when they were old and weak and the girls did not want their bodies any longer, they might become mission teachers. The Brothers had fought that heresy in the Solomons and it was their intention to fight it also in New Guinea.

A young man listening at the Martyrs School had been loud in expressing his intentions to use his education to follow a career that would bring him big money. He thought over the Brothers' talks and then told Bishop Hand that he had changed his plans and wished to go to St Aidan's College. The Bishop urged him not to act on what might be only an emotional impulse but to think the matter over. He did — for the six weeks of the vacation — and when the Bishop's launch came down the coast, gathering up the students for St Aidan's, the new recruit was waiting on the beach at Wanigela.

The church at Eiwo stood on a small plateau on the far side of the Kumusi River. In the wet seasons the river could be crossed only by a precarious cane suspension bridge. The station had been opened after the war by a former pupil teacher of Henry Holland. Then the Reverend George Ambo built the majestic Church of St David. In Passion Week 1957 the church at Eiwo was born when 234 catechumens were baptized. In 1965 Eiwo was two days' walk from Popondetta but only a ten minutes' flight because it now had an airstrip. The district was in many ways a model one. Education, medical assistance and guidance were given to Christians and heathen alike. The district was marked by the generous giving of the people and Eiwo was very largely self-supporting.

But the Reverend John Sharpe was worried by the ignorance of the people as to what happened to their gifts. He felt there was needed more of the spirit of the small Sunday school boy who refused to drop his penny into the collection plate. "Don't you want to give your penny to Jesus?" he was asked. "Yeah," came the answer, "but how're you going to get it to Him?" The priest drew on the school blackboard striking diagrams, showing by the size of the bags how much keeping the mission boarders cost, what went in building materials, wages for the Papuan and white staff, medical, school and travelling expenses. He drew bags to represent how much was received by the annual envelope and church offerings. Then he called a meeting of the elected representatives of the church at Eiwo and its seven out-stations and held the first meeting of the Eiwo District Church Council. He explained how their gifts were first sent to the Bishop, who gave them back so that the priest might pay for wages and stores. When the priest asked for more money, the Bishop sent what he could from what the A.B.M. had given him, until his box was empty, when he went south and begged for more money.

The church councillors were horrified. In eloquent Orokaivan they told of their shame that the Bishop should have to beg money to educate their children. The talk went on, lunch and tea were missed out, and the councillors went away resolved to hold further meetings. These were held, long meetings in traditional church council style: "Father," said one old gentleman to Bishop John Chisholm, "our heads are going round and round," There was a natural reaction in some of the villages against "coming off the dole"; but the Papuan sense of pride, the fear of shame, won out. Christianity was not a cargo cult. At the 1967 meeting of the Australian Board of Missions the Chairman announced that he had that day received a cheque for $200 from Duncan Tiwekuri, Secretary of the Eiwo Church Council, for the Board's funds.

At Koke the Franciscans were worried by the confusion caused among Papuans by the increasing number of religious groups in the capital city. They sought to promote an interest in steps towards Church unity. The Franciscans' dismay was upheld by the older missionary bodies, whose criticism of the unrestricted flow of strange religious sects into Papua did not come from religious intolerance. There was concern over the bewilderment of the native people at the sometimes aggressive "soul-snatching" of the new arrivals, and sadness at the spectacle of a divided Christian Church. The old principle of separate territorial responsibility had been well understood by the Papuans, and had worked effectively for seventy-five years. Understanding, mutual respect, co-operation, had been the policies of the missions in Papua.

The Government Reports of 1963-4 for Papua and New Guinea listed thirty-six different denominations — there had been five before the war — and these new denominations had unusual names. There were the Fitzgerald and O'Shannessy Mission with two non-indigenous missionaries and a hundred followers, Kwato Extension Inc. with eight non-indigenous missionaries, six indigenous ones and 6,290 adherents, and Papuan Holdings (Bailbara) Limited with no missionaries and 500 adherents. In the Sepik area there were the Sola Fide Mission, the New Guinea Gospel and the Christian Missions in Many Lands.

In June 1965 the Australian Council of Churches sent a team on an ecumenical visit to Papua and New Guinea. The seven officers visited typical mission stations of their own, the Roman Catholic and other churches. They interviewed officers of the government and Members of the Assembly. In their report it was stated that of the 2,000,000 Papuans 1,250,000 were Christians. The section of the report dealing with the preparation of cate-chumens showed a wide variety of practice, and some may be concerned as to how great the veneer of Christianity may be in certain cases. The Lutherans insisted on two to three years in a catechumen class, the Papua Ekalesia required one year's training, with a shorter time in special cases. The Methodists asked for six months in the catechumens' class, following a personal decision for Christ and acceptance by a Leaders' Meeting and baptism. The Anglican Church required "hearers" to be enrolled for a period of two years and during that time to attend special classes outside the church. Then followed attendance in the catechumens' class for another two years. After that came baptism, when they

K

took their place as members of the Church, normally to attend a confirmation class for a further year before being admitted to full membership.

The report discussed a "withdrawal of expatriate staff" as a process that must go on constantly in a world of developing nations. It commented that in New Guinea–Papua the withdrawal was "almost without exception" upwards. The missionary handed over ground level work and supervised while carrying out more specialized tasks. Local staff are advanced step by step, and ultimately the missionary withdraws from all responsibilities at village or elementary level. Few missionaries, it was claimed, were found working alongside or under local staff at the lower levels. "This has the effect of depreciating the value of the calling to serve at village level. It promotes ambitions for advancement or preferment in the local worker in terms of rising in the scale of postings and getting clear of service in the village."

The report suggests that the alternative to "withdrawal upwards" was "withdrawal sideways", where the expatriate specialist and the local trainee are paired in undertakings. When the expatriate withdraws, his local counterpart is in full swing.

The 1967 Staff List for the Diocese of New Guinea offers an interesting commentary on the suggestion of the Ecumenical Committee. At twenty-one stations, expatriate and indigenous clergy are working together. Whether the "withdrawal sideways" will be of the expatriate or indigenous staff is another matter. At sixteen places the staff listed is entirely expatriate; six of these might be regarded as positions of responsibility to a white community, the remainder would be front-line mission stations. The committee's recommendation does carry with it some overtones of a white superiority, which is not assumed by the Anglican Mission. There are stations where ordained Papuan clergy hold senior positions to the white staff, and stations where the Papuan priest-in-charge has obviously been chosen for years of faithful service. In the highlands, in the Managalas, there is scarcely any occasion for talk of withdrawals except to advance posts of greater missionary hardship. The pioneer work again appears to be done, as this record shows, by white or Papuan evangelists, by the Melanesian Brothers (of whom there are now twenty in New Guinea), or by a combination of all three as the situation requires.

Sakarina in the Managalas area of the Owen Stanleys is only a hundred miles from Port Moresby. It is accessible only by air or by walking, for there are no roads. It was an area troubled by the confusing teachings of sects operating from Port Moresby, but the people felt that their affinity lay with the Anglican Mission to the north. From there came the medical patrols of Sisters Henderson and Vesperman, their Papuan teachers and medical evangelist, and the teacher who produced a primer in their vernacular — Brother Philip of the Society of St Francis.

In 1961 the Reverend Bevan Meredith established the mission station in its present form, with church, school, boys' and girls' dormitories, playing-fields, workshop, clinic and hospital. There are now a dozen out-stations and schools, a staff of three Europeans and forty-five Papuans.

On the eve of St Andrew's Day 1966 occurred a baptismal service which was the reward of five years of instruction. Four hundred and fifty adults were baptized, with European and Papuan priests standing in the water to receive them from their sponsors. Clad in clothes with striking Managalasi designs, the people moved in procession to St Columba's Church, singing New Testament phrases in the local language, using local music patterns. The significance of the occasion lies partly in the fact that here, a hundred miles from the sophisticated life of Port Moresby, was a community so primitive that it was but a short time since the first Managalas woman had been confined in a small bush hospital. Supplies for Sakarina mission are brought by plane from Eroro, where they are landed by the mission's boats St Columba's School has an enrolment of three hundred children and education goes to Standard VI. There is no government school educating an élite; but roads and bridges are matters of great importance to the elected Members of the Legislative Assembly, and it will probably not be long before a road is made to the Managalas.

The region bears to Port Moresby a similar position to that of the eastern highlands of New Guinea to Lae. From Lae to Goroka and on to Mount Hagen there is a road, and access from parts of the highlands to the town is comparatively easy. In Lae, with a large expatriate white population and with the removal of tribal sanctions on the native people, venereal disease has reached alarming proportions; the *treated* cases number one in eighteen patients at the hospitals. To Lae also highland girls have come in numbers to form a prostitute community.

If there has been a tendency for the Bishop of New Guinea to space out his senior staff and assistant bishops, it is because the Anglican Mission has to face new problems. At a mission such as Sakarina the staff may be called upon to run a bank, a trade store, supervise the airstrip, or maintain machinery. They are not coffee planters, builders, mechanics or bank officers, storekeepers or agricultural experts, but if the Anglican Mission's policy of educating the Papuan into his community is to be maintained, if the drift to the towns is to be checked, these things must be done by the white and Papuan staff.

The postings of the assistant Bishops show a strategic placing throughout the diocese. Bevan Meredith is at Madang, the back-door to the New Guinea highlands, George Ambo is at Popondetta, the coffee-drying depot in Sister Brenchley's time, which is now an Administration centre, Henry Kendall is at Dogura. David Hand, Bishop of New Guinea, has moved from the historic cathedral seat of Dogura to Port Moresby, the capital. It is desirable that the Department of Territories, the trading class, and the Legislative Assembly, the technical and teachers' college and officials, should be aware of the existence of the Anglican Mission and its work north of the Owen Stanleys in an area avoided alike by academic research workers and the writers of tourist books.

The 1967 Conference was the first of its kind. Under the new interim constitution, clergy, lay men and *women* shared responsibility in the conduct of the diocese. The conference produced some vigorous discussion from the indigenous delegates. It faced the agonizing problem of how the Anglican Mission could, after three-quarters of a century of free education to the Papuan, carry on her school system efficiently and reach the required standards on the meagre assistance granted. Would some of the outer schools have to be closed: the schools where the need for education was greatest? The schools that could not as yet reach the "standard required for government registration", a requirement that could not be reached either by government or mission teachers as yet in some districts. Would there have to be a reduction of children in other schools because there were not enough fully trained teachers? The answers to these questions must depend upon the response of the Department of Territories, the Legislative Assembly of Papua–New Guinea, and teachers in Australia or the United Kingdom who may see the work of teaching in a struggling country as one for which financial remuneration is not the ultimate reward.

At the 75th Anniversary Celebrations held in Dogura there was on St Laurence's Day a microcosm of the history of the Anglican Mission to New Guinea. On the shore at Kaieta, where Albert Maclaren and Copland King landed, a shrine was dedicated by the Primate of Australia, the Most Reverend Philip Strong, Archbishop of Brisbane, and Bishop of New Guinea for more than one-third of the history of the Anglican Mission. An address was given by the eighty-seven-year-old Canon Peter Rautamara, one of the first two Papuan priests. He, the Reverend Edwin Nuagoro and Bernard of Wamira alone remain of the Wedauan tribesmen who stood on the beach on that windy day in August 1891, when the whaleboat drew near the shore.

At the Cathedral of St Peter and St Paul there were over a thousand communicants, and four Papuans were ordained to the priesthood, the sign of an ever stronger indigenous Church. Greetings were brought by representatives of the government, other parts of the Anglican Communion, the Roman Catholic, Lutheran, Papua Ekalesia and Methodist Churches.

The new frontiers of highlands and the towns must be faced; but at Dogura, spiritual power-house of the Anglican Mission, the traditions of a Church woven into the life and customs and dress of the Papuan people would be preserved. In an evening spent in feasting, singing, speeches, dancing, a great procession wound about the cathedral with drums, the servers moving with unconscious dignity, the voices rising in wild native chants and terrific volume, with banners, incense, and vestments figured with native patterns. When the indigenous and expatriate clergy and teachers, medical workers and builders, went back to their isolated stations, they would be fortified by the thought of the daily routine at Dogura, the bell which would ring three times a day for service and the hundreds who would silently glide into the Cathedral to pray for those absent or in any kind of need.

In February 1968 from the Mambare River, that region served

for so many years by Copland King and Romney Gill, a cheque for $18.65 came to Sydney for the Freedom From Hunger Campaign in Asiatic countries. The cheque, signed by Japhet Kolbua, Cecil Okono, and Stephen Yawota, was from the Mamba District Church Council. "We have very little money but we are seldom hungry as our gardens and sago from the swamps provide plenty of food." The teaching of the years had borne its fruit.

APPENDIX A

Beginnings of the New Guinea Mission

THE MINUTES of the meetings that established the New Guinea Mission are preserved at the Federal Office of the Australian Board of Mission, Stanmore, Sydney.

The minutes of the meeting held at the Diocesan Registry, Sydney, on 21st December 1886 with the Most Reverend the Primate in the Chair, contain an agreement whereby it was requested that the Primate should communicate with the Society for the Propagation of the Gospel and the Church Missionary Society with a view to raising £1,500 per annum for the proposed New Guinea Mission.

The meeting of 28th October 1887, held in St Andrew's Chapter House, stated that the Primate reported that the Society for the Propagation of the Gospel in Foreign parts had written that it had opened a special fund for the New Guinea Mission and would make a grant for two years of £500 per annum. "The Secretary also read a letter from the Reverend W. Gray, one of the secretaries of the Church Missionary Society expressing regret at the inability of the society to give any help."

Both sets of minutes are confirmed by the signature of "Alfred Sydney".

The minutes of the meeting held on 1st October 1889 at the Chapter House, Sydney, record the acceptance of the offer of A. A. Maclaren to proceed to New Guinea. His letter dated 17th June 1890 is gummed into the minute book.

On 10th October 1890 the question of episcopal superintendence of the New Guinea Mission was discussed, and it was agreed that this should be exercised not by the Bishop of North Queensland, but by the Primate. The Reverend A. A. Maclaren was interviewed and stated that in the first case he had offered himself to the S.P.G. but "He now regarded himself as under the Board of Missions and would be willing and happy to recognize the Primate as his director".

The Most Reverend the Primate was in the Chair, and at the next meeting two months later the minutes of the meeting of 10th

October were confirmed by the signature of "William Saumarez Sydney".

The Diocese of Sydney holds a unique honour, and responsibility, for the New Guinea Mission.

APPENDIX B

Letter from the Reverend Vivian Redlich to his father.

THIS letter is now held in St Paul's Cathedral, London:

Somewhere in the Papuan Bush,
July 27th, 1942.

My dear Dad,

The war has busted up here. I got back from Dogura and ran right into it — and am now somewhere in the parish trying to carry on, though my people are horribly scared.

No news of May and I'm cut off from contacting her — my staff O.K. so far but in another spot.

I'm trying to stick whatever happens. If I don't come out of it just rest content that I've tried to do my job faithfully.

Rush chance of getting word out, so forgive brevity.

God bless you all,

VIVIAN

APPENDIX C

From Wanigela to Abau

WANIGELA lies eighty-five miles south-east of Gona and fifty miles from Eroro. When the decision was made to stay even in the event of Japanese invasion, the Reverend Dennis Taylor prepared for the necessity to "go bush". He divided a reserve of foodstuffs into three portions, each sufficient to serve for three months' rations, and hid these in the bush and in one of the villages.

The aim at Wanigela mission was to preserve a normal life for as long as possible for the hundreds who looked to the staff for guidance and help. School, dispensary, the church services, continued with planes passing frequently overhead. Air-raid drill was instituted by Father Taylor.

Japanese planes at first took little notice of the mission; then came an American airman who had parachuted from a B-26 plane, which had run out of petrol, and who had spent nineteen days wandering about. He was followed by an ANGAU officer returning from inland patrol. The officer brought with him the Reverend R. L. Newman of Eroro, who had brought his wife to Wanigela and had been returning to his own district when he found it occupied by the Japanese.

The ANGAU officer had with him armed constables disguised as village men, and gathered much information about the Japanese invasion at Gona and Buna. His report was that the Japanese were advancing on Kokoda, that all white men in the north were marked for death, and that scouts were being sent out in search of Europeans in hiding. He referred to the assistance given to the Japanese by Embogi, the Papuan sorcerer who had been bribed with an Emperor's Ring and the promise of a high position when the Japanese became masters of New Guinea. The police-scouts told of having seen themselves the Japanese offering and withdrawing food to Mavis Parkinson and May Hayman when they were imprisoned in the coffee house.

It is possible that the ANGAU officer knew of these executions and of those on the beach at Buna, but he would have been under bond of secrecy until he made his report. He did hint at the possibility that the two girls were killed. He than gave orders that the Wanigela mission station should be evacuated by the staff immediately. He would provide two armed constables to conduct a party over the Owen Stanley Range. The men could return to the district when they had seen the women to safety. The officer spoke of cruelty on the part of the Japanese to any natives who helped or harboured any white, and of the methods used to extract information from those unwilling to betray their friends. He urged Father Taylor to take the women out of the area as quickly as possible.

Two mornings later, on 29th August, the party which included Mrs Taylor, her young baby, Mrs Newman and Sister Dorothea Tomkins set out. There were forty volunteer carriers for the first three-day stage of the journey to the foothills. Here a depot was being established in the care of Father Newman and Brother Salzmann. Baggage for the remainder was cut by Father Taylor to a minimum: pillow, rug, mosquito net, tins to last so many days, a couple of lamps, a billy can and saucepan. Trade tobacco was of great importance, for with this the party could buy supplies of food and hire carriers when beyond the influence of the mission. The responsibility upon Father Taylor was very great, but his cheerfulness and consideration greatly encouraged the three women, whether they were trudging along a stony river bed, or climbing with hands and toes dug in up a steep mountainside. The route taken was completely unexplored. On the top of the Owen Stanleys the coldness stung the fingers and toes of the women, whose footwear was now in tatters. The descent on the southern side was easier and took less time.

When he had safely delivered the three women and the baby into the care of responsible men, Father Taylor went down with fever for three days. He then immediately made his way back to Abau and over the Owen Stanleys to the depot held by the missionaries in the foothills south of Wanigela.

APPENDIX D

Letter from Father James Benson

Holy Cross,
Friday even.

My dear. . . .

I am fit and well again and have already done a few jobs. Father Lester, Godfrey, George, Sister, everybody send their love to you. . . .

Lots of things I had intended to say to you & forgot. One rather important is about candles for the Altar at ———. I found the custom was to get out 8 new candles every Sunday & Holy Day & then the halves & quarters were put into a box — which you see opposite the bathroom — and apparently that was the end of them.

I issued orders that no new candles are to be put out until all
these are used. The longest for Sundays & the stumps for week-
days & I explained that to throw a candle into a box and leave it
for the cockroaches and rats to eat is an insult to a good candle.
Once a candle has been lighted to the glory of God it must be
allowed to burn itself out in His praise. That is the whole reason
for lighting them. Each one is a parable of human life & the ——
practice is as though a boy were allowed to praise God until he was
18 and then be put in a box, snuffed out, to be covered with cob-
webs and devoured by rats, or as at —— in the vestry, by fowls.
. . . All this of course is quite apart from the question of economy.
Important though it is I consider it secondary here. . . .

Index

DATE DUE

HIGHSMITH 45-220